GUITAR TAB 2014 2015

ISBN 978-1-4950-1252-5

HAL•LEONARD®
CORPORATION

7777 W. BLUEMOUND RD. P.O. BOX 13819 MILWAUKEE, WI 53213

Visit Hal Leonard Online at
www.halleonard.com

$34.95

Allons-y (1)

Music by David Gilmour

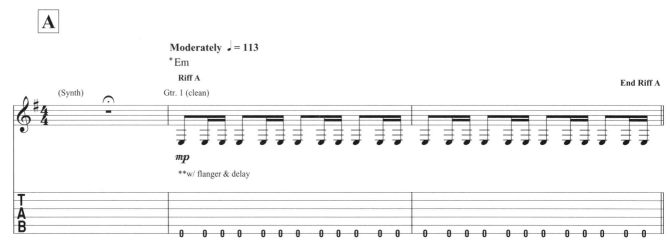

*Chord symbols reflect overall harmony.
**Delay set for dotted eighth-note regeneration w/ 1 repeat.

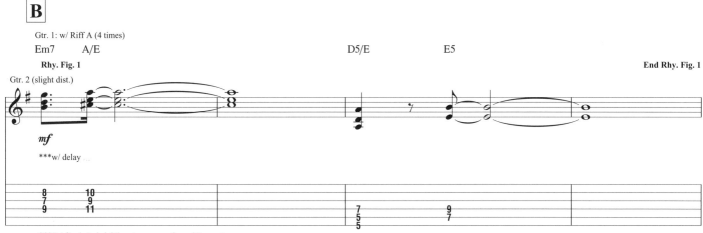

***Set for dotted eighth-note regeneration w/ 5 repeats.

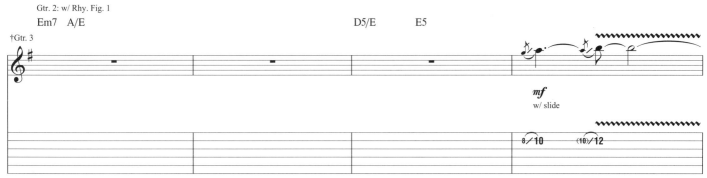

†Lap steel gtr. arr. for gtr.

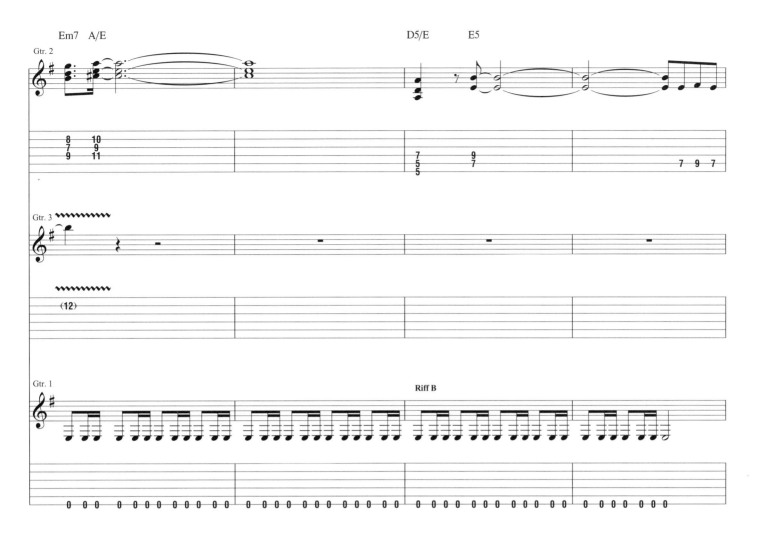

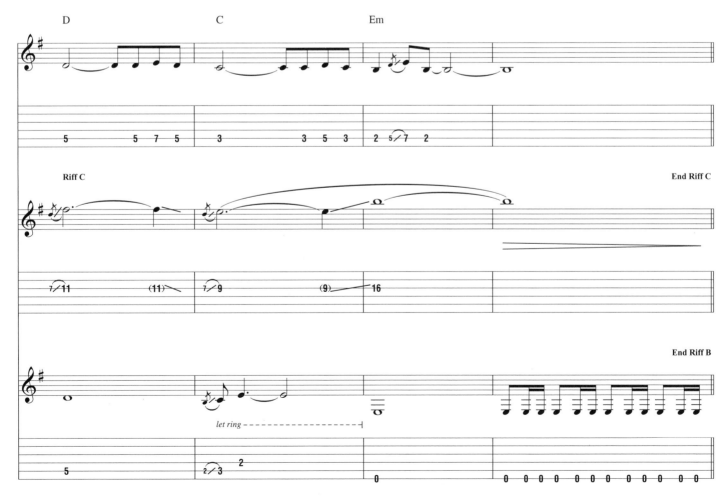

Gtr. 1: w/ Riff A (5 times)
Gtr. 2: w/ Rhy. Fig. 1 (2 1/2 times)

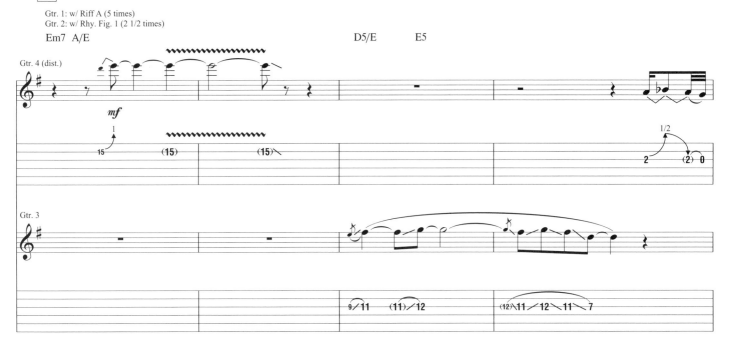

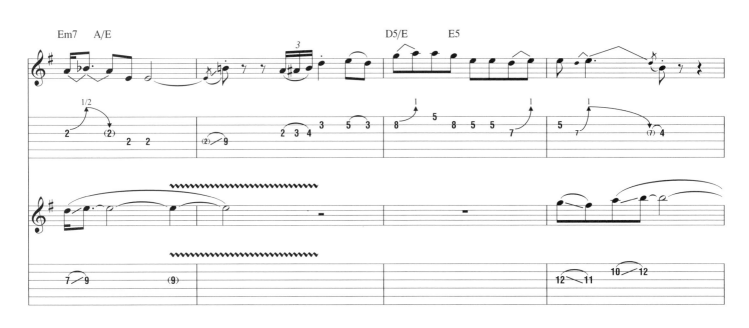

Gtr. 1: w/ Riff B
Gtr. 3 tacet

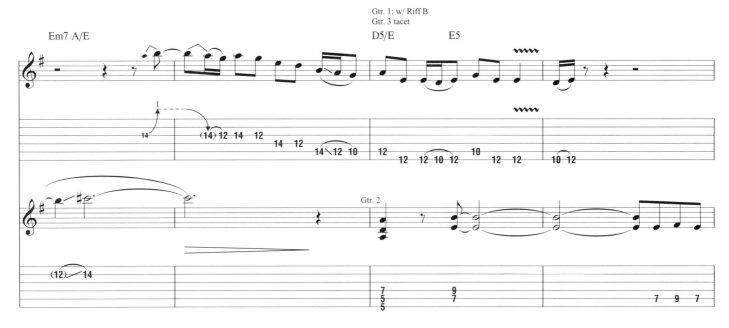

4

Gtr. 3: w/ Riff C

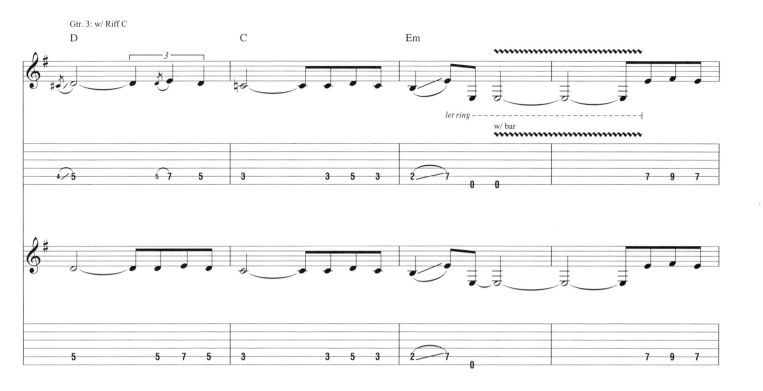

Gtr. 1: w/ Riff B (last 4 meas.)

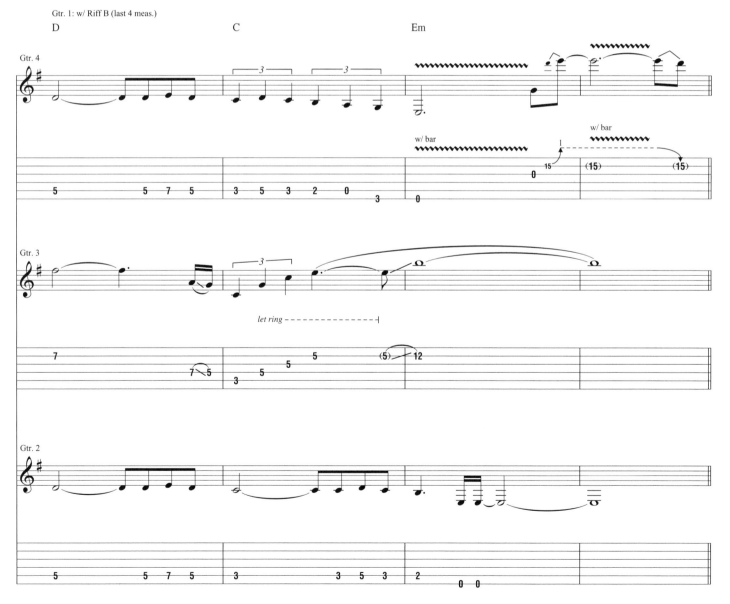

from Maroon 5 - *V*

Animals

Words and Music by Adam Levine, Ben Levin and Shellback

*Chord symbols reflect overall harmony.

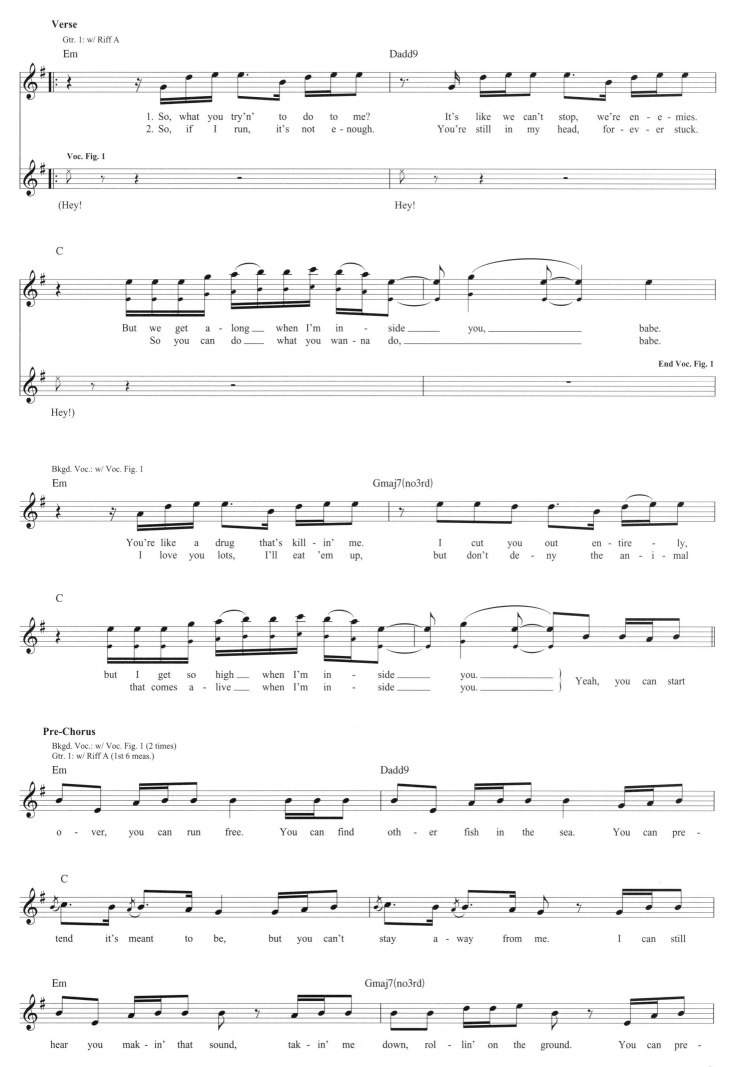

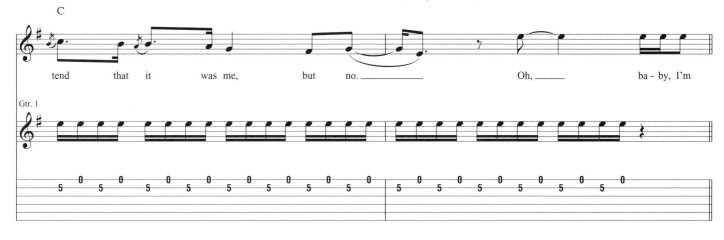

2nd time, Gtr. 1: w/ Fill 1

tend that it was me, but no. _____ Oh, _____ ba - by, I'm

Gtr. 1

§ **Chorus**

Gtr. 1: w/ Riff A
3rd time, w/ Bkgd. Voc. ad lib (next 14 meas.)

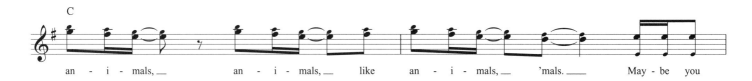

prey - in' on you to - night. _____ Hunt you down, eat you a - live _____ just like

an - i - mals, _____ an - i - mals, _____ like an - i - mals, _____ 'mals. _____ May - be you

think that you can hide. _____ I can smell your scent for miles _____ just like

an - i - mals, _____ an - i - mals, _____ like an - i - mals, _____ 'mals. _____ Ba - by, I'm...

Bridge

Gtr. 1: w/ Riff A
2nd time, Gtr. 1: w/ Riff A 1st 6 meas.)

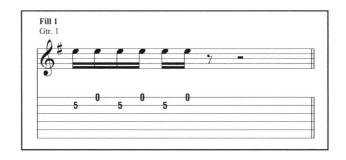

Don't tell no lie, lie, lie, lie. _____ You can't de - ny, 'ny, 'ny, 'ny _____ that beast in - side, side, side, side. _____

Fill 1
Gtr. 1

w/ Bkgd. Voc. ad lib (next 2 meas.)

Em   Gmaj7(no3rd)

___ Yeah, ___ yeah, yeah.   No, girl, don't lie, lie, lie, lie. ___ You can't de - ny, 'ny, 'ny, 'ny ___

C

___ that beast in - side, side, side, side. ___   Yeah, ___ yeah, yeah.

Interlude

N.C.

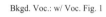

Yo, _____ oh,   uh, whoa, _____ oh, oh. _____   Whoa, __

Bkgd. Voc.: w/ Voc. Fig. 1

___ oh, oh. ___   (Just like an - i - mals, _ an - i - mals, _ like an - i - mals, _ 'mals. _ Just like

D.S. al Coda
(no repeat)

Yeah, _____ yeah, _____ yeah. _____   Ba - by, I'm
an - i - mals, _ an - i - mals, _ like an - i - mals, _ 'mals.) _   Ow! _____

⊕ Coda

C

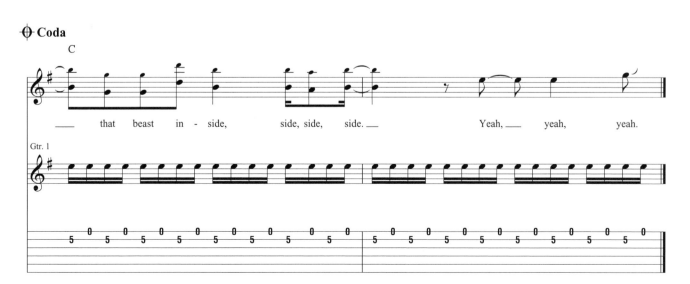

___ that beast in - side, side, side, side. ___   Yeah, ___ yeah, yeah.

Gtr. 1

The Devil in I

Words and Music by Corey Taylor and James Root

Drop D tuning, down 2 1/2 steps:
(low to high) A-E-A-D-F♯-C♯

Intro
Very fast ♩ = 175

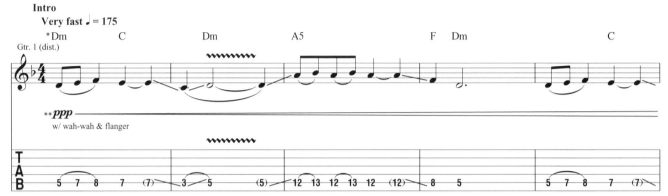

*Chord symbols reflect implied harmony.
**Track fades in.

***Set for one octave below w/ 25/75 wet/dry ratio, and fade from 25% to 75% saturation over next 2 meas.

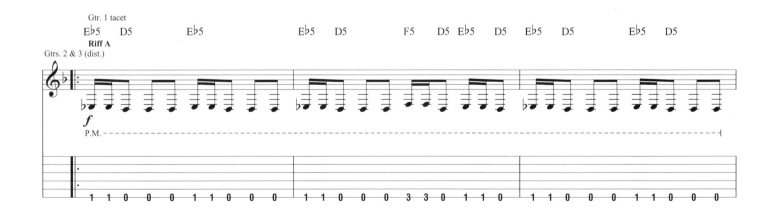

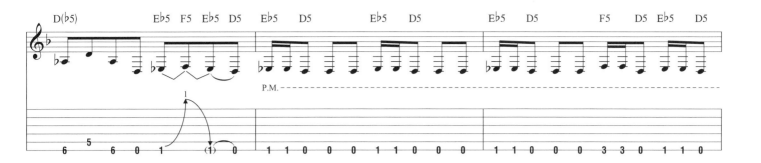

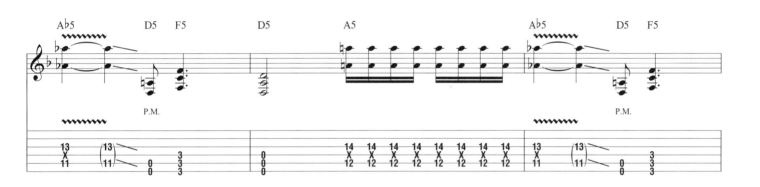

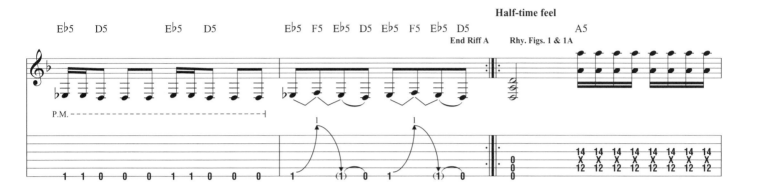

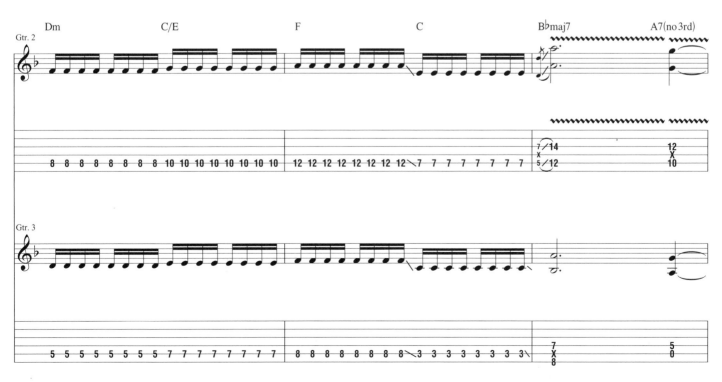

*Pick sixteenth-notes and produce random harmonics by lightly touching the 6th string
and gradually sliding the fret-hand in the direction indicated in tab.

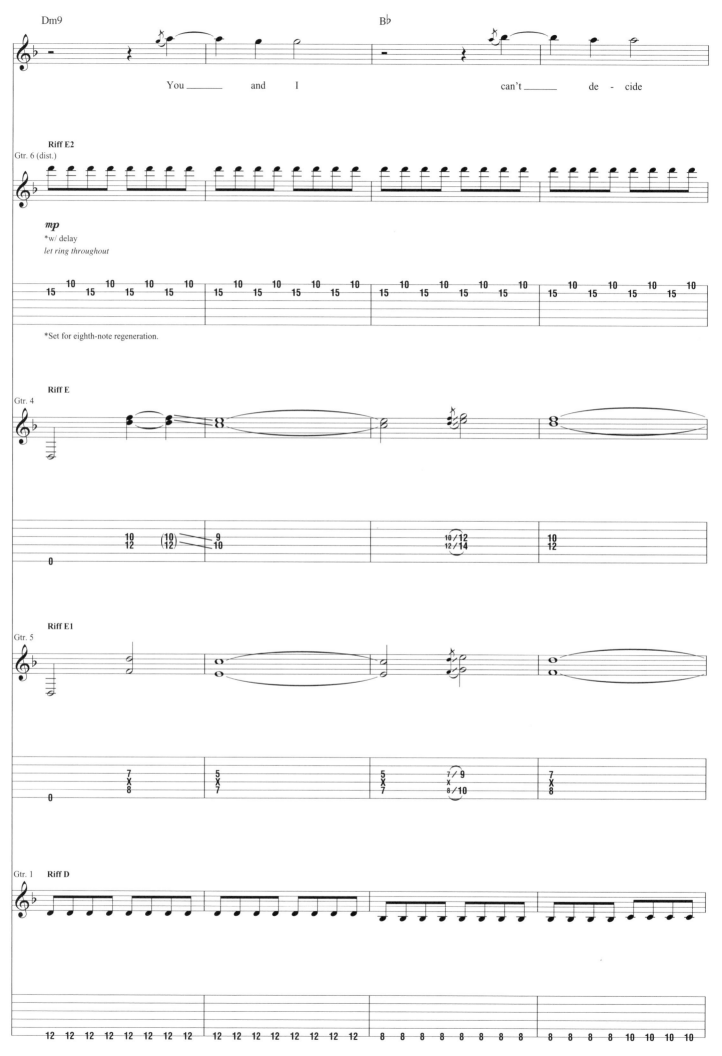

You _____ and I   can't _____ de - cide

Verse

Gtr. 1: w/ Riff C (2 times)
Gtrs. 2 & 3: w/ Rhy. Fig. 2
Gtrs. 4 & 5: w/ Riffs B & B1 (2 times)

2. Un - der ___ the words ___ of ___ men,

some - thing ___ is tempt - ing ___ the fa - ther.

Where is ___ your will, ___ my ___ friend?

In - sa - ti - ates, ___ nev - er e - ven both - er.

Gtr. 1: w/ Riff D (2 times)
Gtrs. 4, 5 & 6: w/ Riffs E, E1 & E2

You _____ and I, _____ wrong _____ or right,

trad - ed _____ a lie for _____ the le - v'rage.

In _____ be - tween _____ the lens _____ in light,

you're _____ not what you _____ seem.

D.S. al Coda 1   ⊕ **Coda 1**

End half-time feel

Gtrs. 2 & 3: w/ Rhy. Fill 1   Gtrs. 2 & 3: w/ Rhy. Fills 2 & 2A

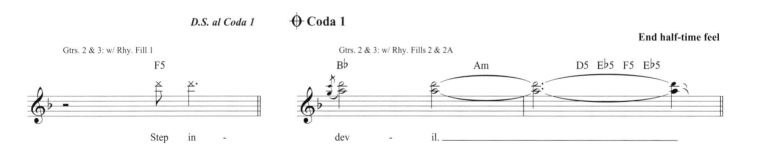

Step in - dev - il. _____

Bridge
Gtrs. 2 & 3: w/ Riff A (2 times)

I'm not your dev - il an - y - more! _____

21

Your sta - tion is a - ban - doned.

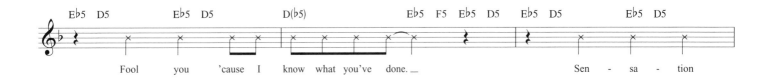

Fool you 'cause I know what you've done. ___ Sen - sa - tion

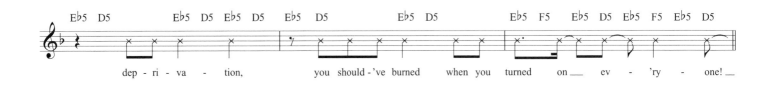

dep - ri - va - tion, you should - 've burned when you turned on ___ ev - 'ry - one! ___

Interlude
Double-time feel

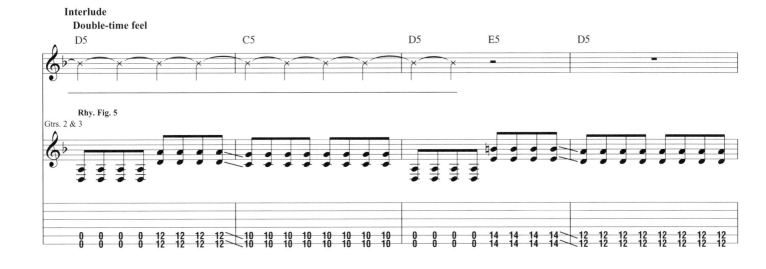

Rhy. Fig. 5
Gtrs. 2 & 3

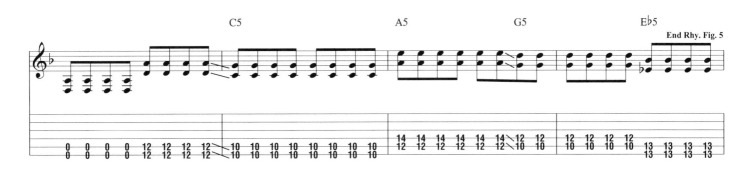

Gtrs. 2 & 3: w/ Rhy. Fig. 5

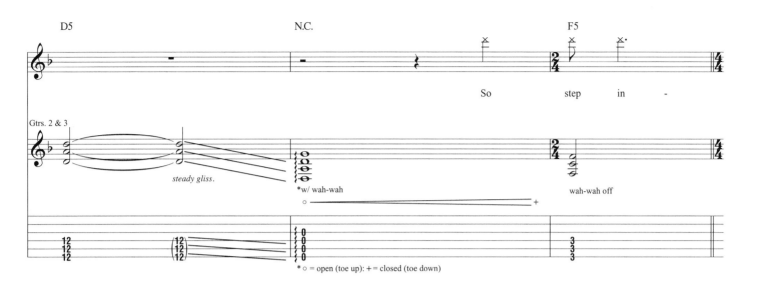

Chorus
Half-time feel

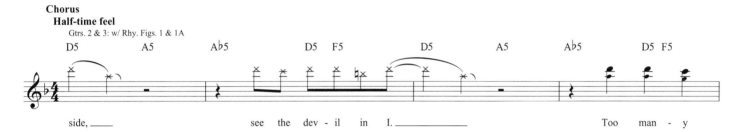

D.S. al Coda 2

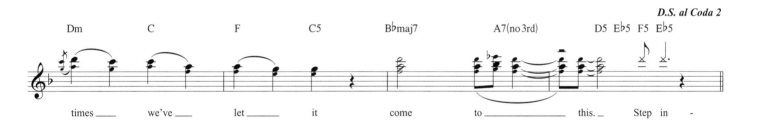

Coda 2

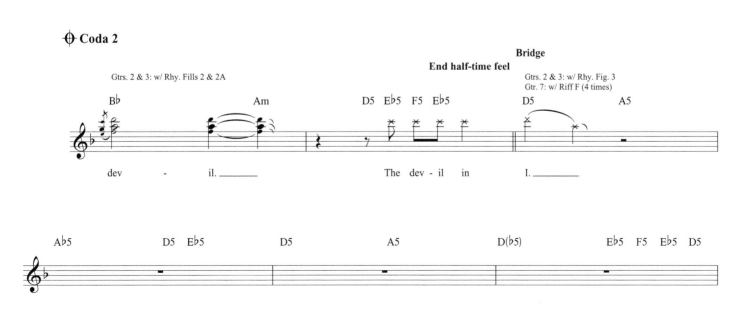

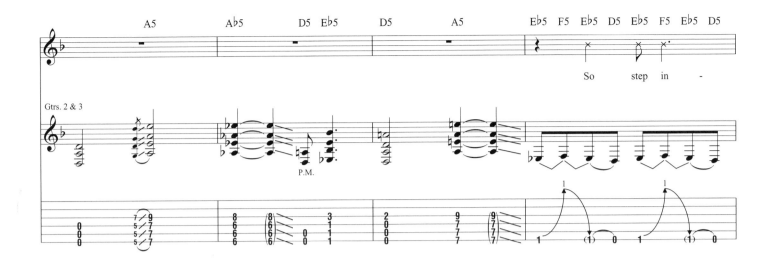

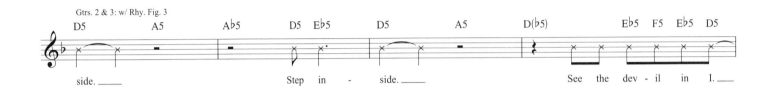

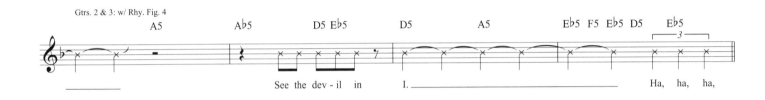

Outro
Gtr. 1: w/ Riff C (3 times)
Gtrs. 2 & 3: w/ Rhy. Fig. 2
Gtrs. 4 & 5: w/ Riffs B & B1 (3 times)

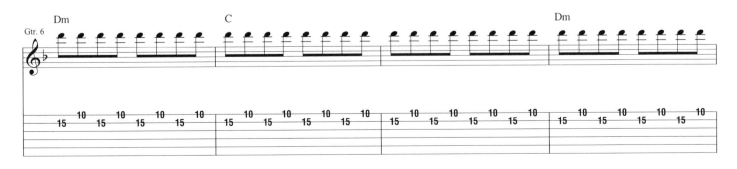

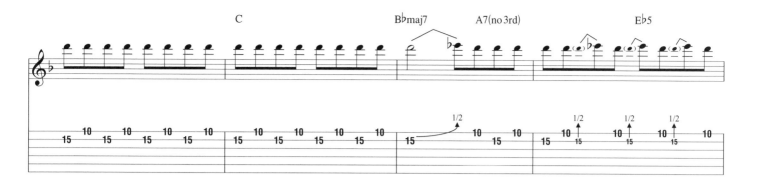

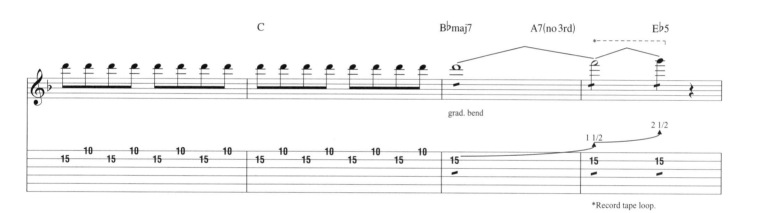

*Record tape loop.

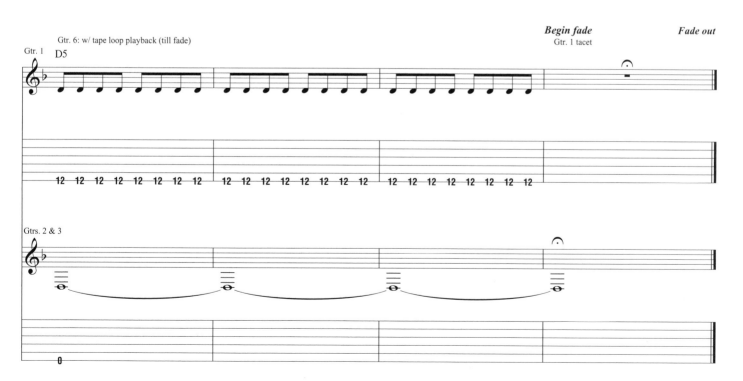

Fever

Words and Music by Dan Auerbach, Patrick Carney and Brian Burton

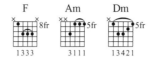

*Bass arr. for gtr. **Chord symbols reflect implied harmony.

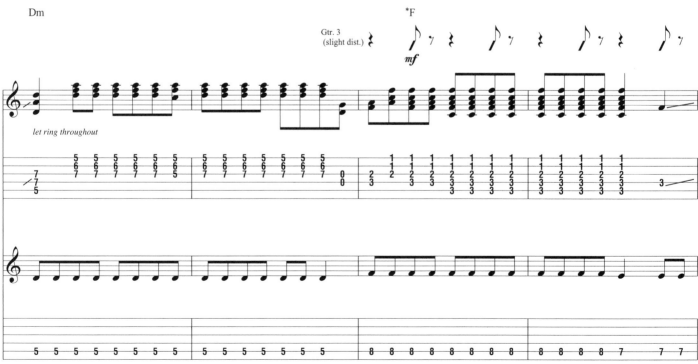

*See top of page for chord symbols pertaining to rhythm slashes.

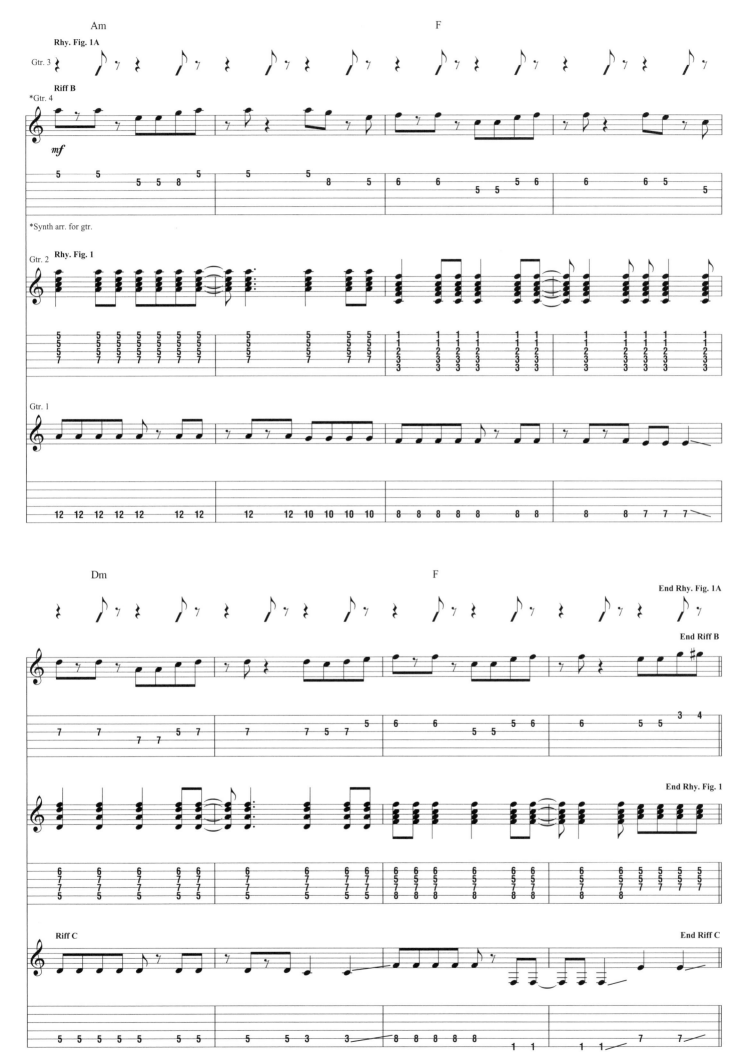

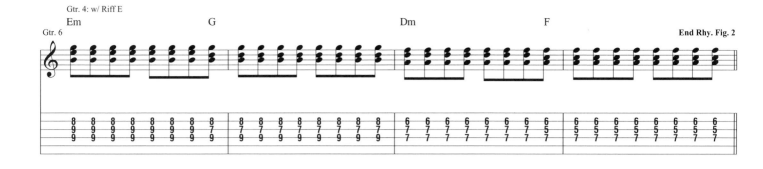

Bridge

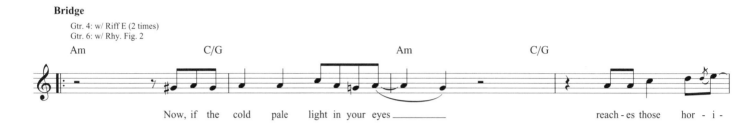

Now, if the cold pale light in your eyes _____ reach - es those hor - i -

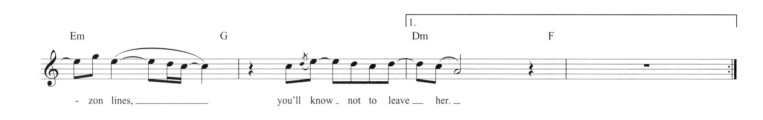

- zon lines, _____ you'll know __ not to leave __ her. __

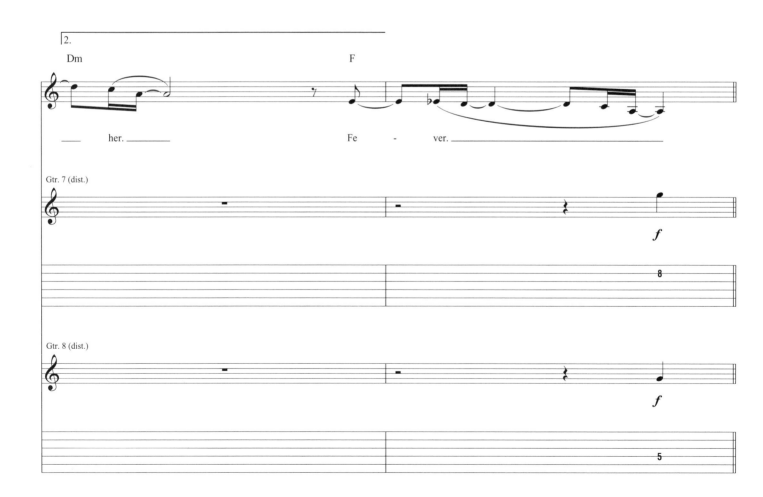

___ her. _____ Fe - ver. __

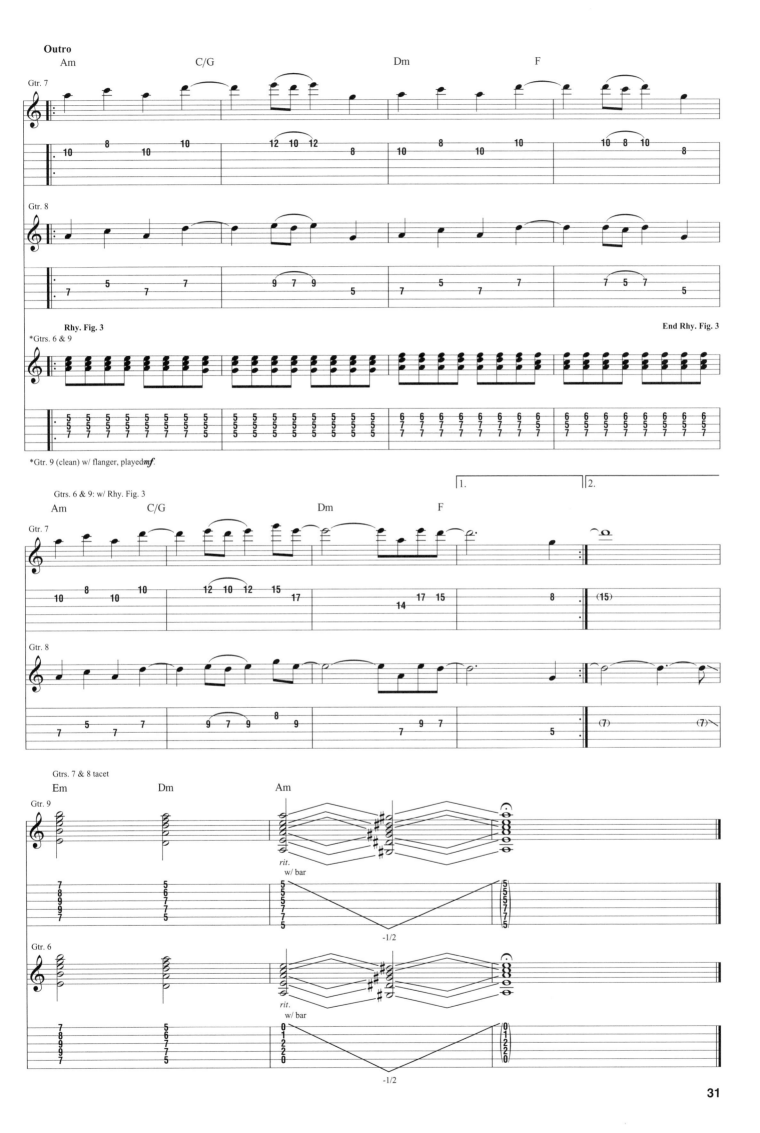

from Mastodon - *Once More 'Round the Sun*

The Motherload

Words and Music by Brent Hinds, Brann Dailor, Bill Kelliher and Troy Sanders

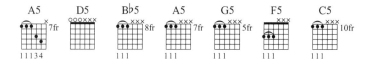

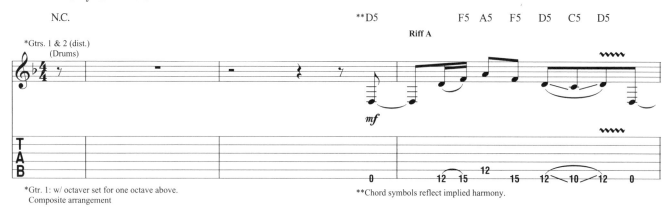

Drop D tuning, down 1 step:
(low to high) C-G-C-F-A-D

Intro
Moderately fast ♩ = 146

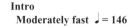

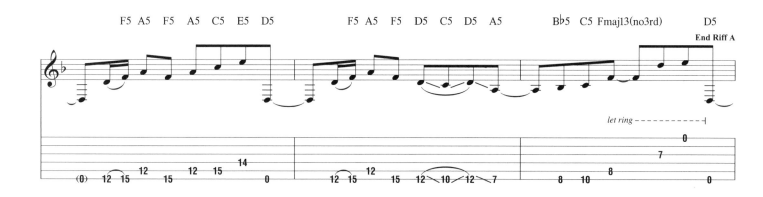

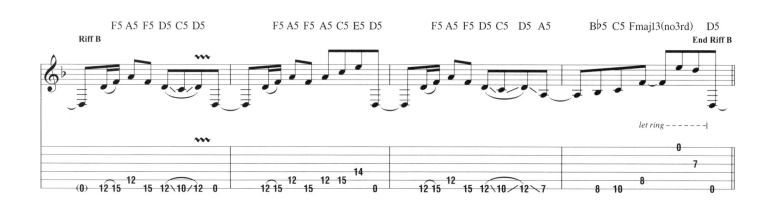

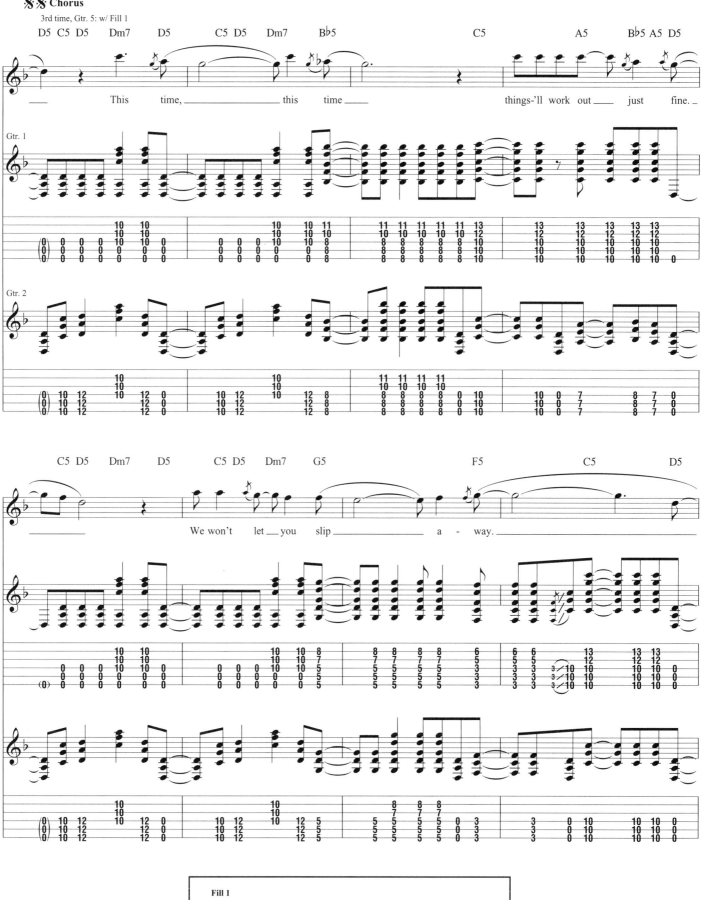

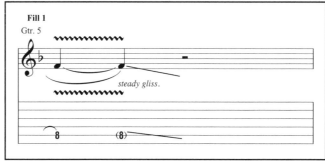

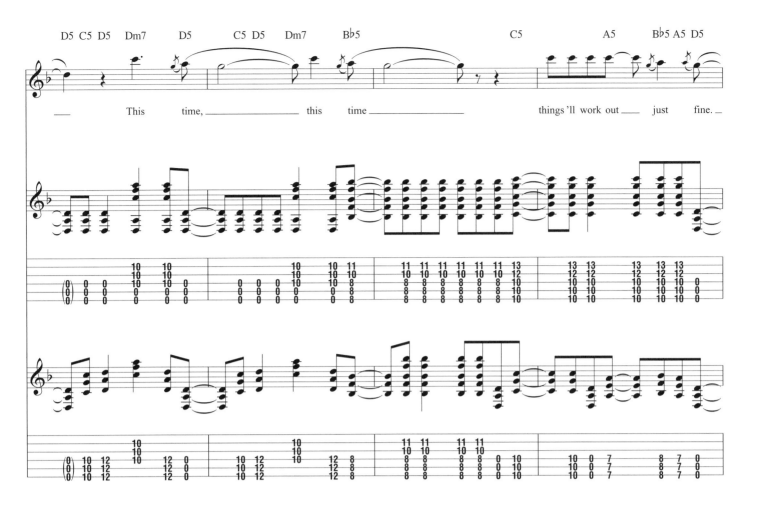

This time, _____ this time _____ things'll work out ___ just fine. __

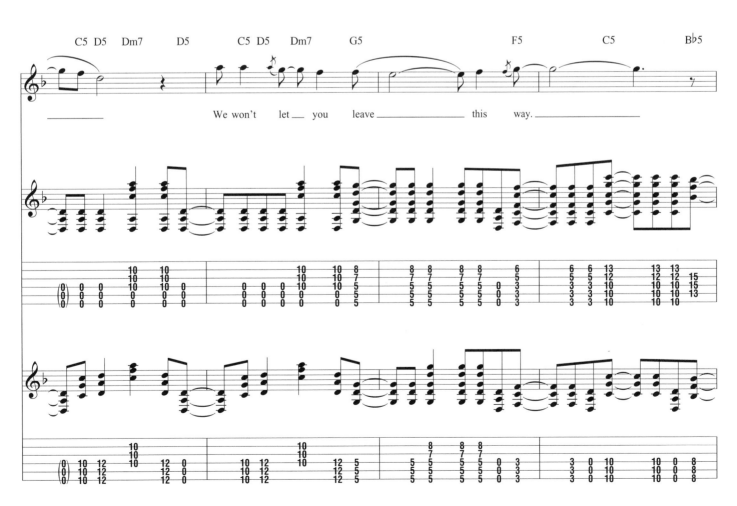

_____ We won't let ___ you leave _____ this way. _____

Gtrs. 1 & 2: w/ Riff C

F5 A5 F5 D5 C5 D5   F5 A5 F5 A5 C5 E5 D5   F5 A5 F5 D5 C5 D5 A5   C5   G5 C5 D5

⊕ **Coda 1**

Interlude

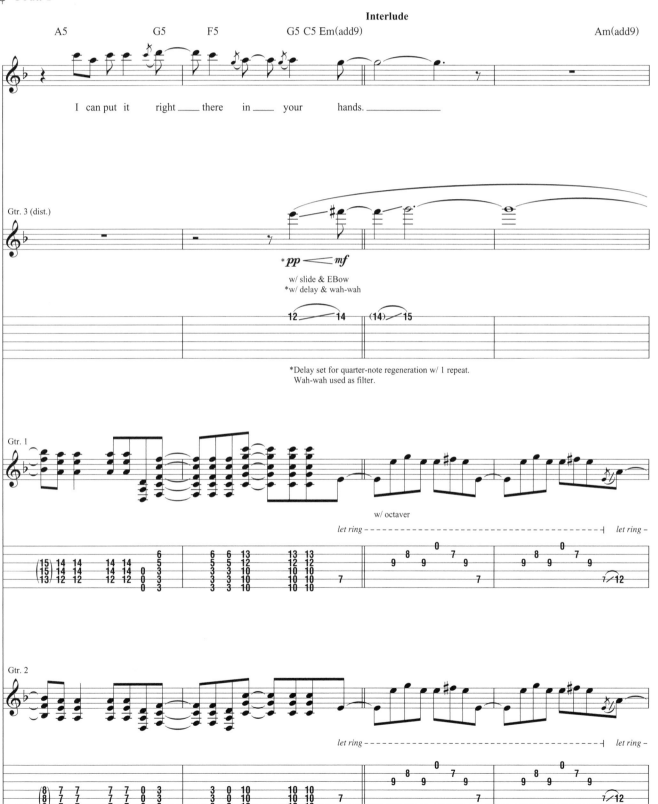

I can put it right ___ there in ___ your hands. _____

Gtr. 3 (dist.)

* *pp* < *mf*

w/ slide & EBow
*w/ delay & wah-wah

*Delay set for quarter-note regeneration w/ 1 repeat.
Wah-wah used as filter.

Gtr. 1

w/ octaver

let ring - ┤ *let ring* -

Gtr. 2

let ring - ┤ *let ring* -

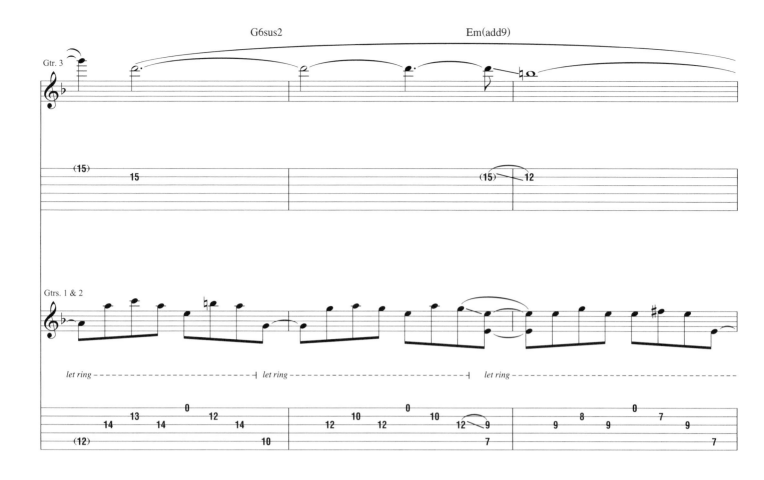

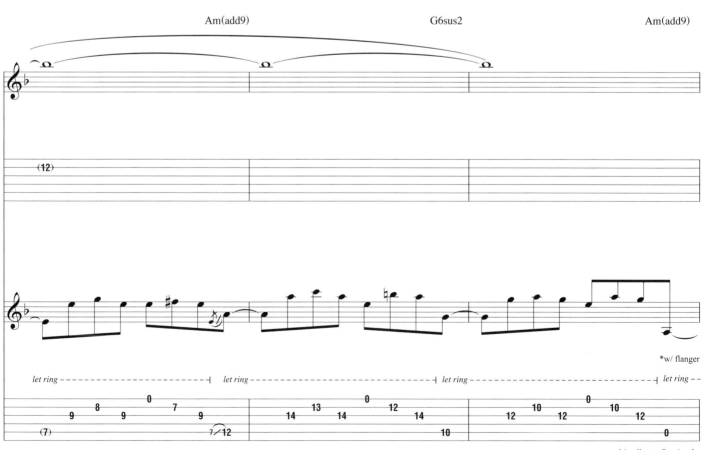

*Applies to Gtr. 1 only.

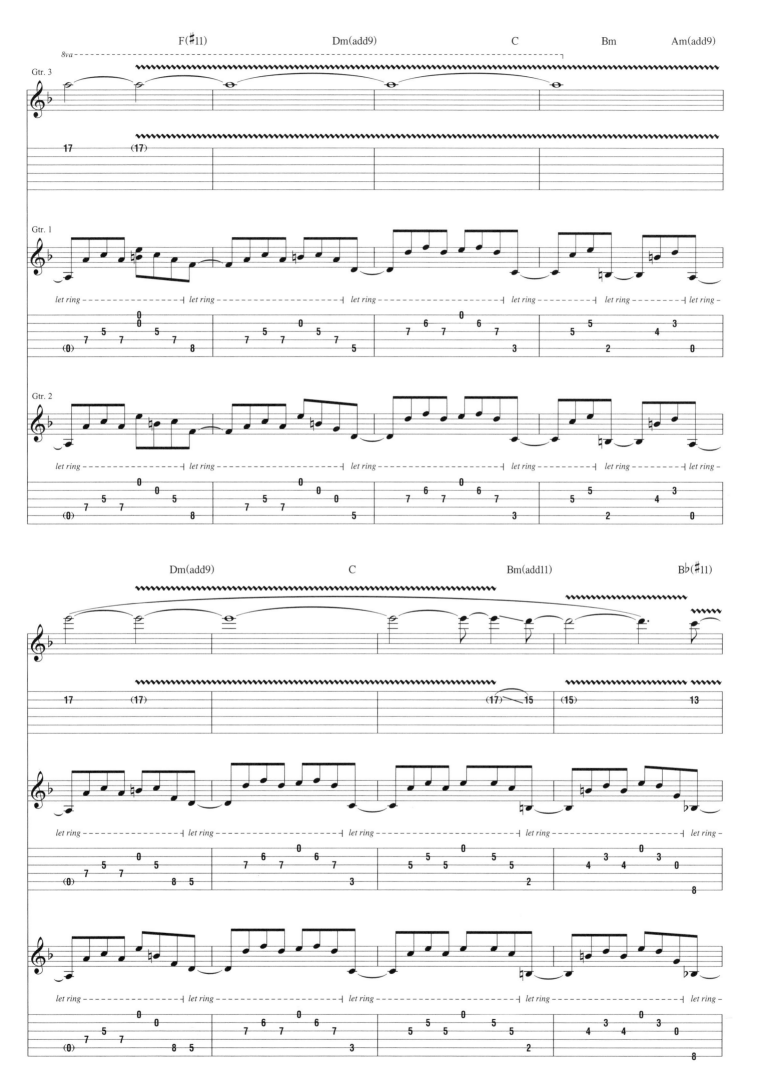

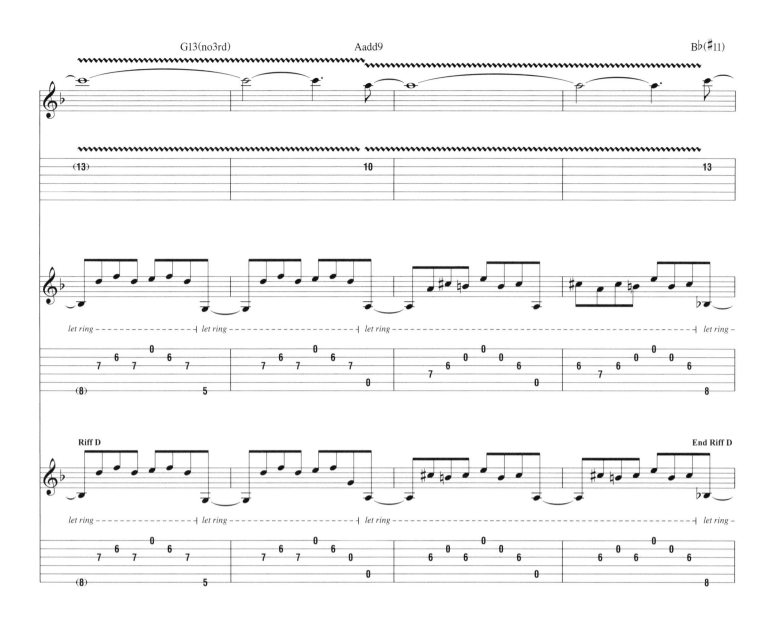

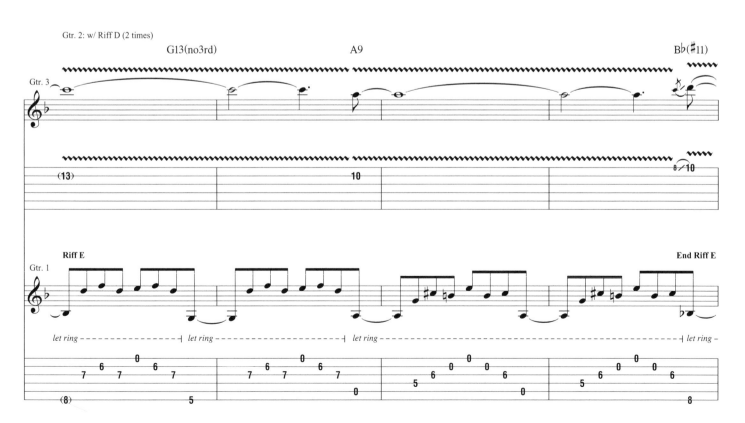

Interlude

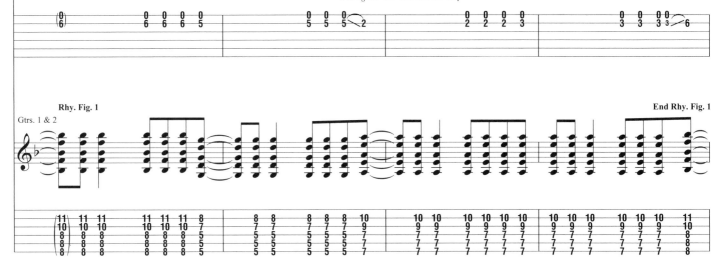

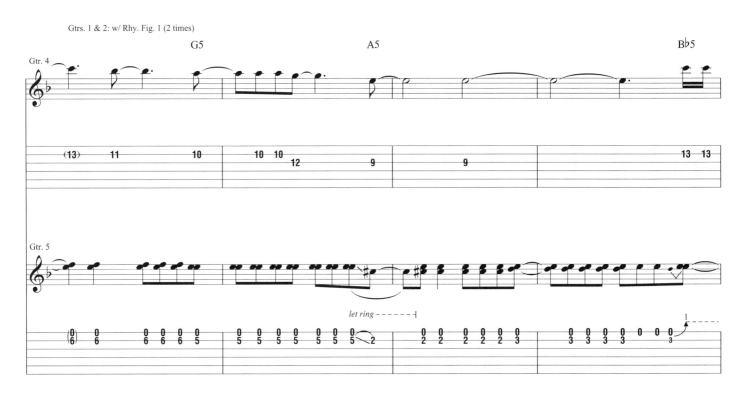

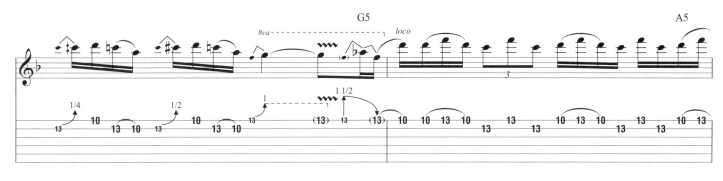

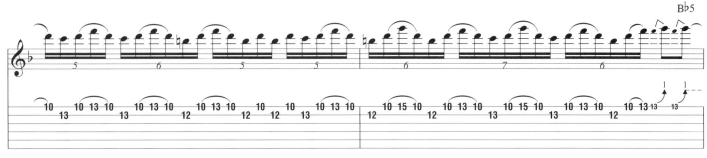

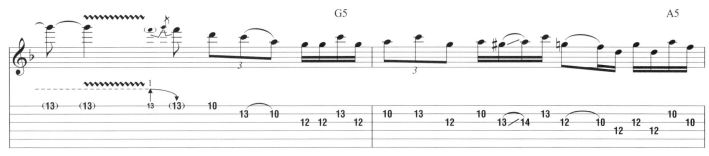

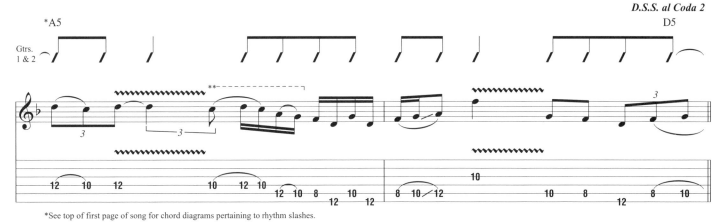

*See top of first page of song for chord diagrams pertaining to rhythm slashes.
**Played ahead of the beat.

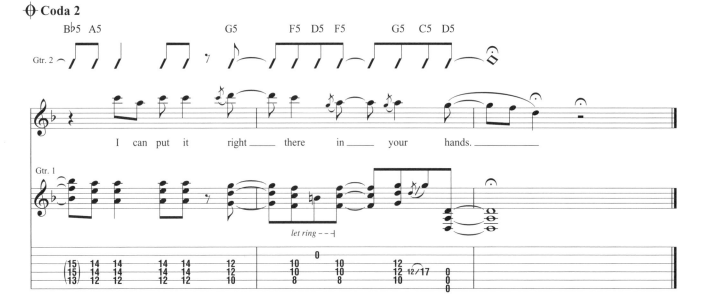

I can put it right____ there in____ your hands._____

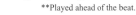

from Joe Bonamassa - *Different Shades of Blue*

Oh Beautiful!

Words and Music by Joe Bonamassa and James House

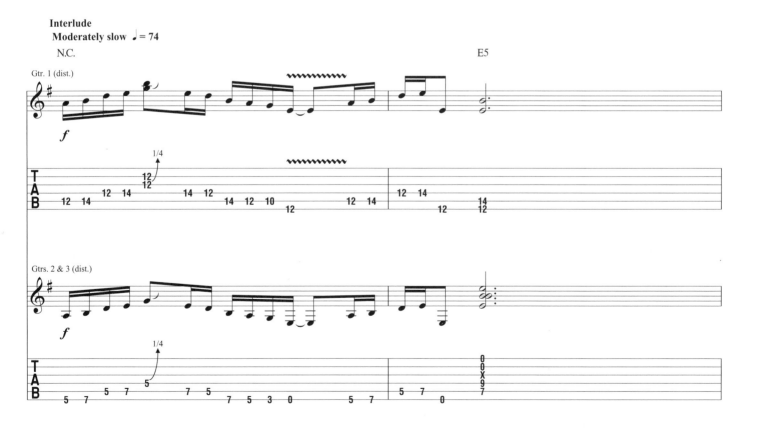

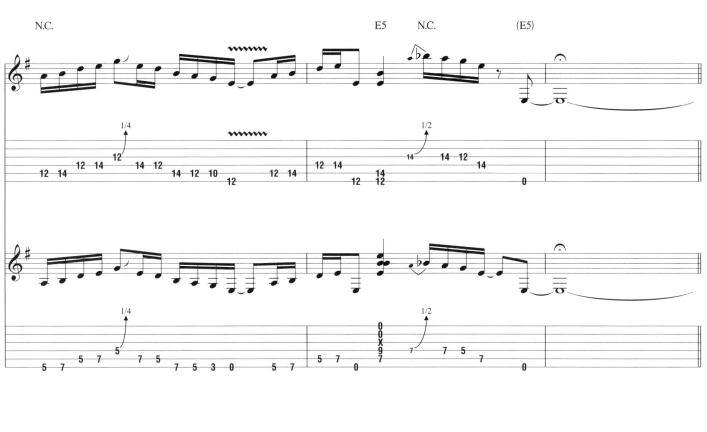

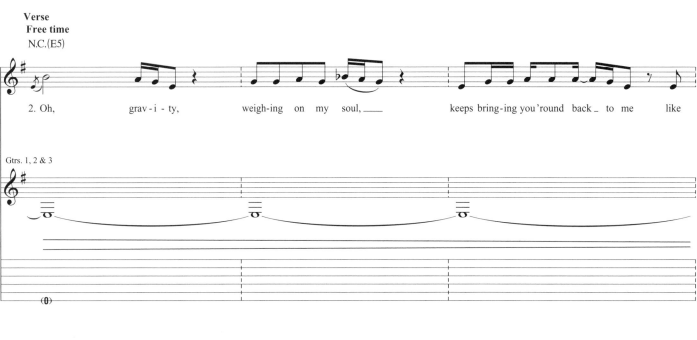

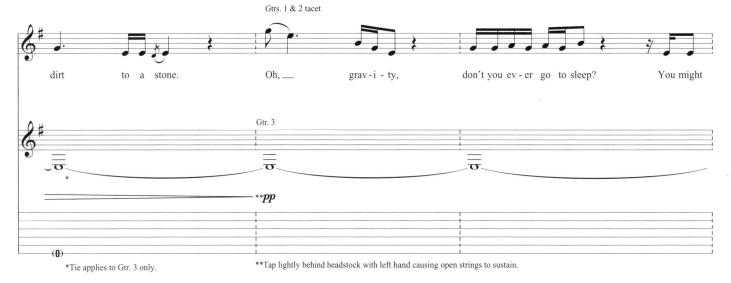

*Tie applies to Gtr. 3 only.   **Tap lightly behind headstock with left hand causing open strings to sustain.

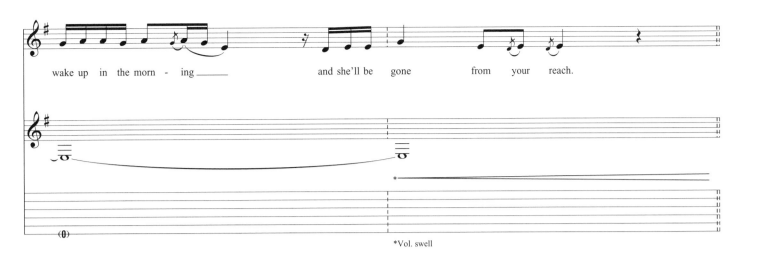

wake up in the morn - ing _____ and she'll be gone from your reach.

*Vol. swell

Interlude
A tempo

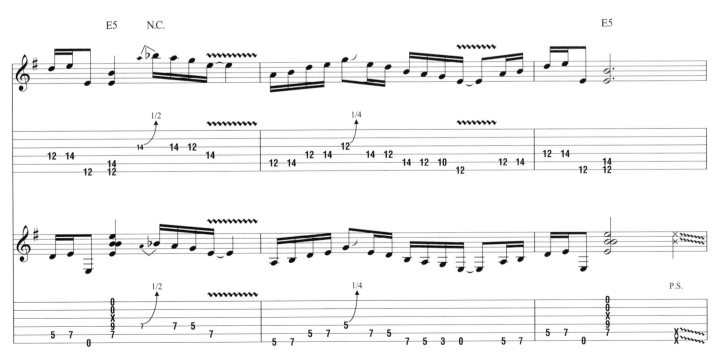

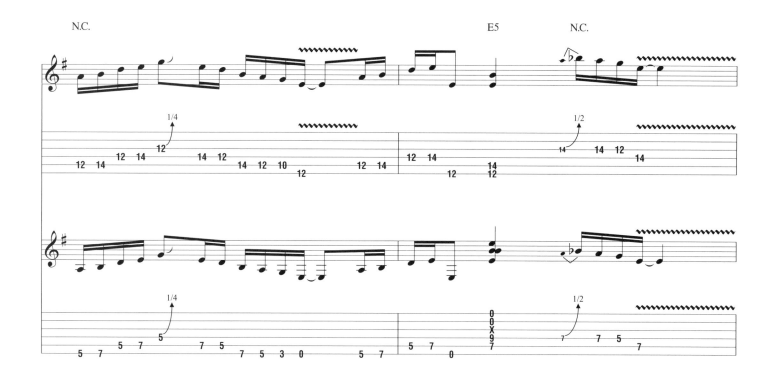

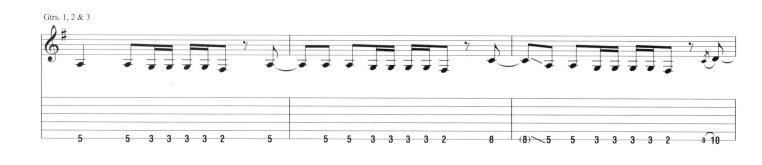

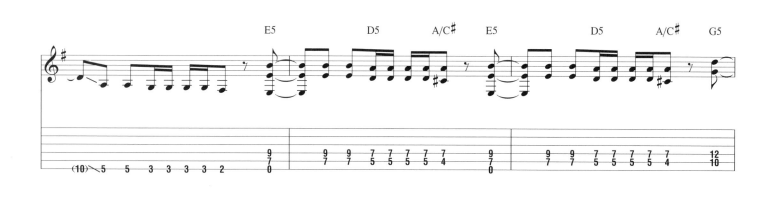

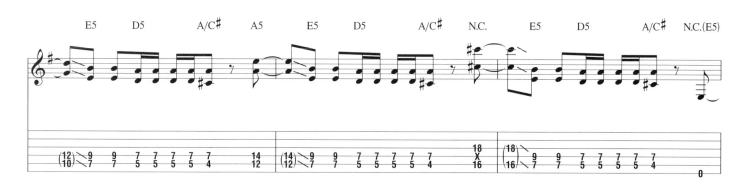

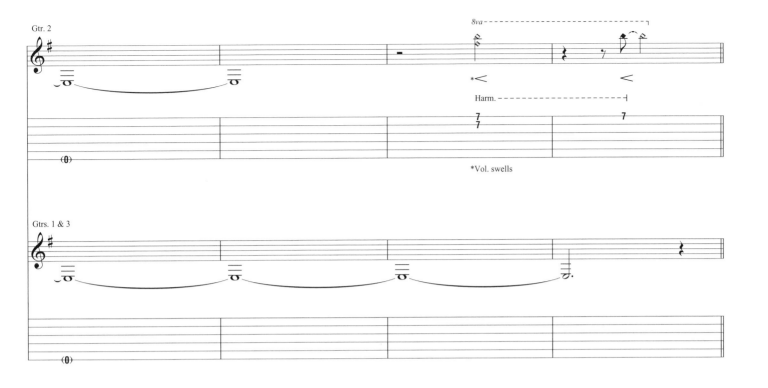

*Vol. swells

Guitar Solo

N.C.(E5)

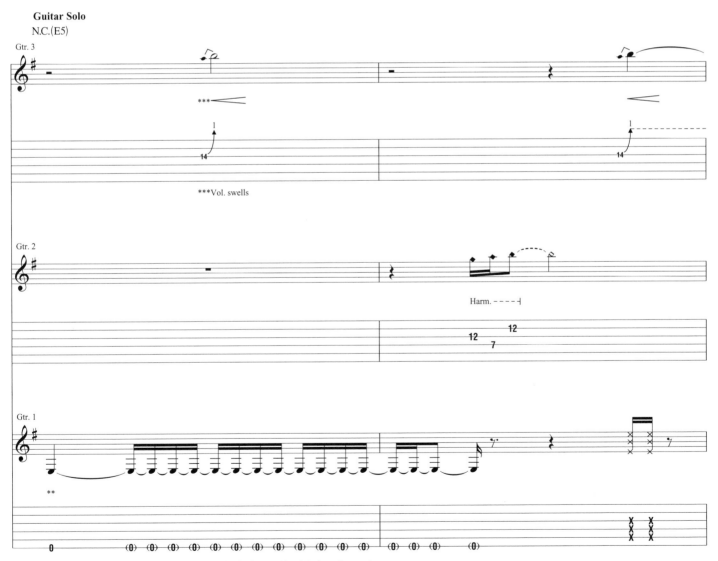

***Vol. swells

**Using a guitar with Les Paul style electronics, set lead volume to 10 and rhythm volume to 0.
Strike the strings while the pickup selector switch is in the lead position,
then flip the switch in the rhythm indicated to simulate the re-attack.

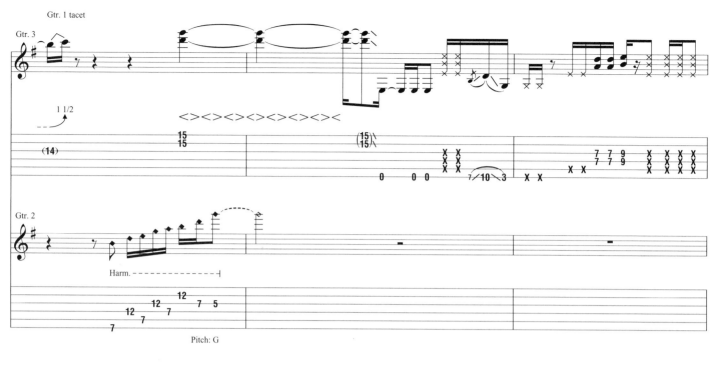

Pitch: G

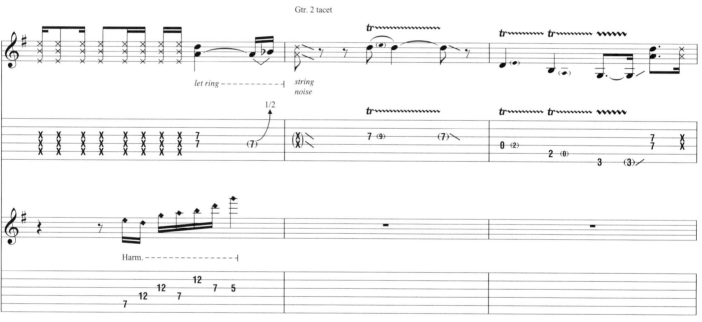

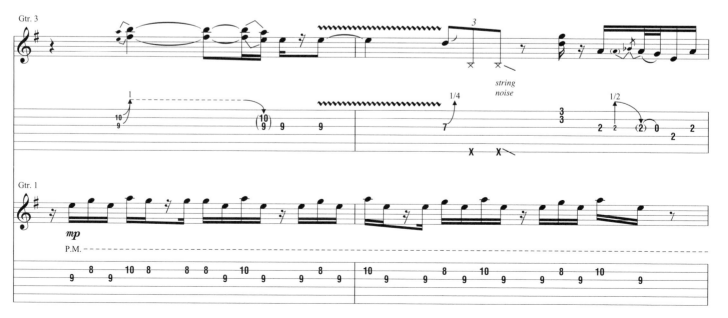

50

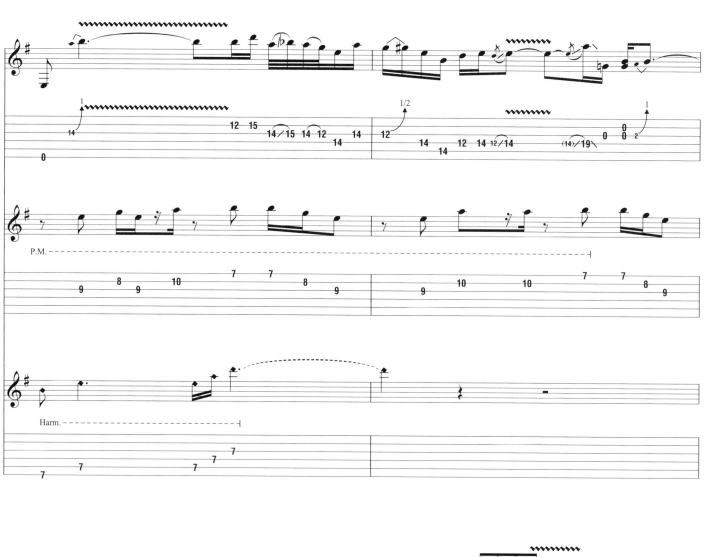

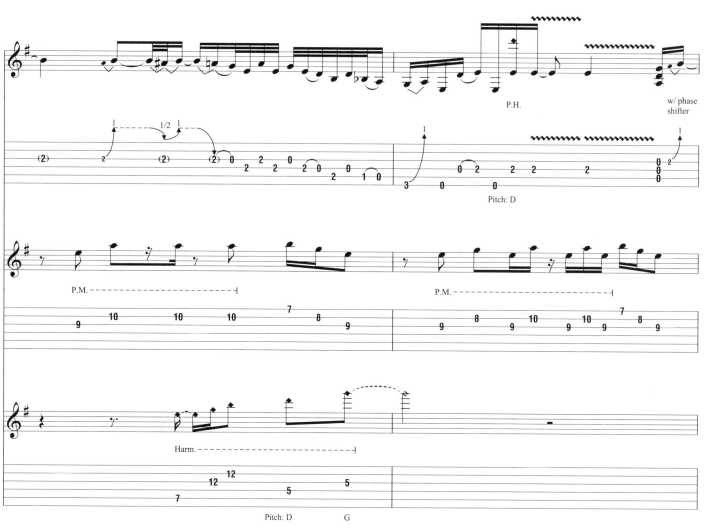

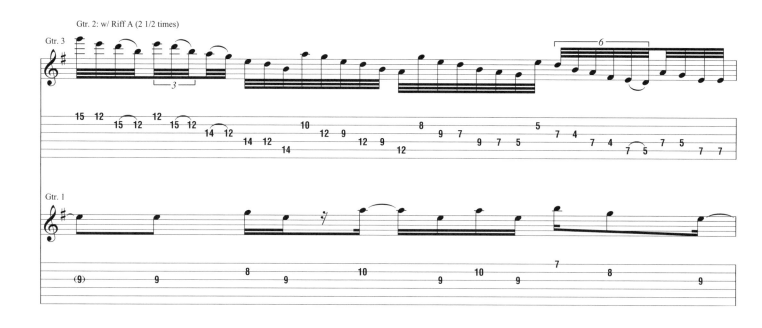

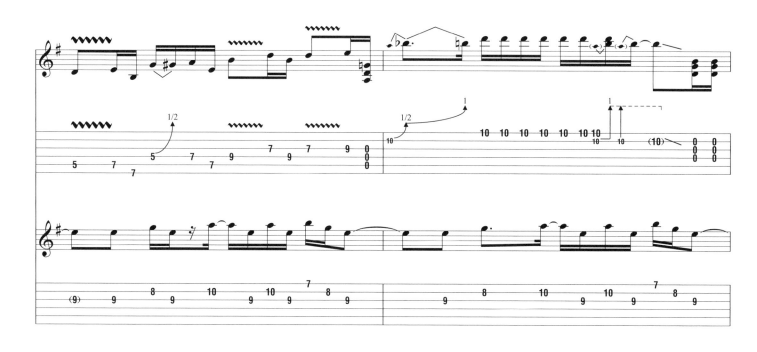

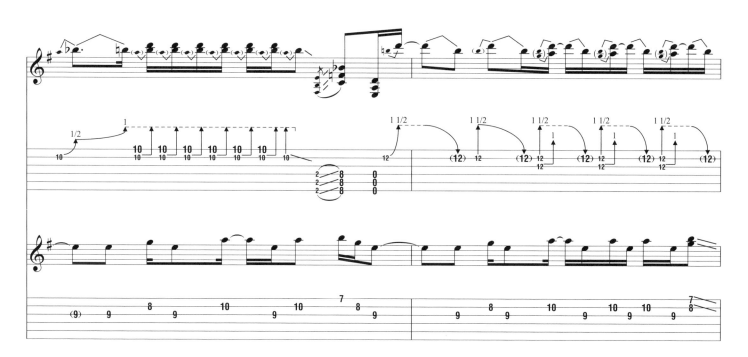

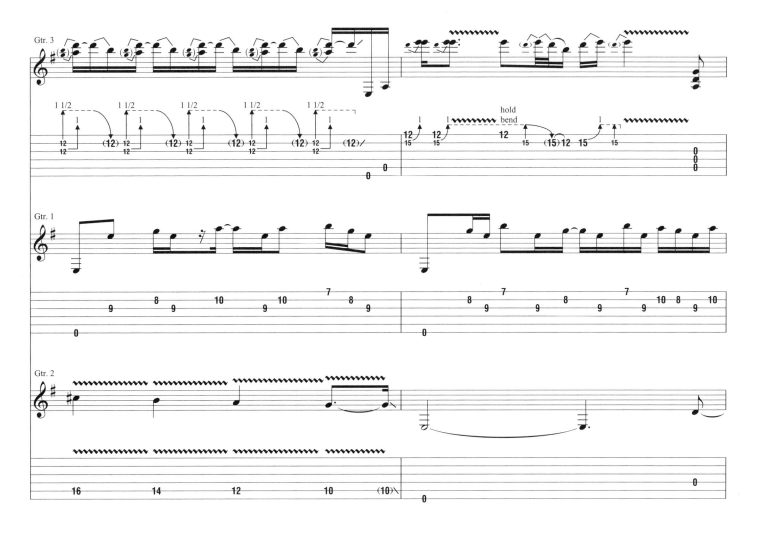

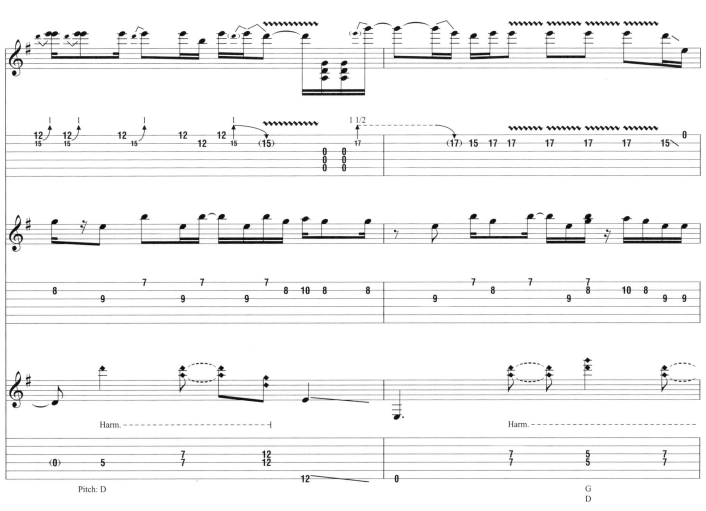

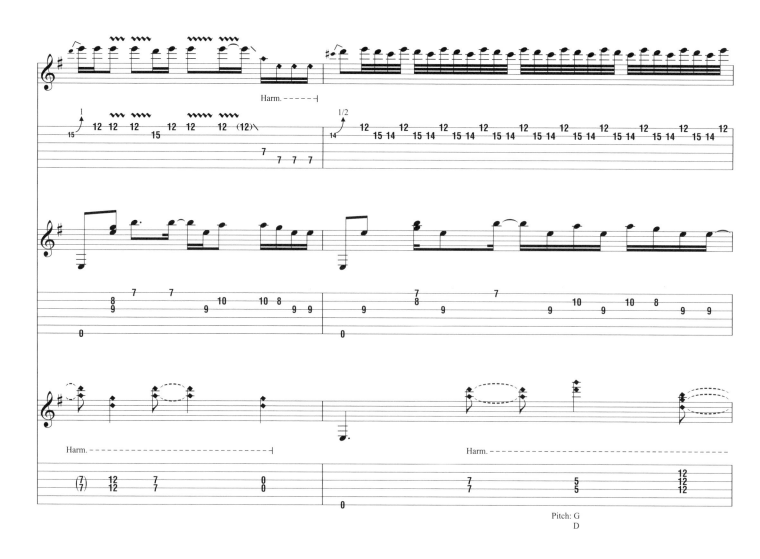

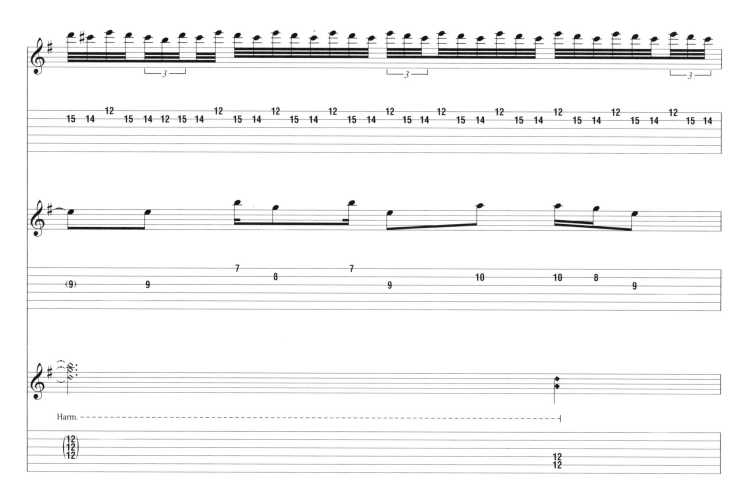

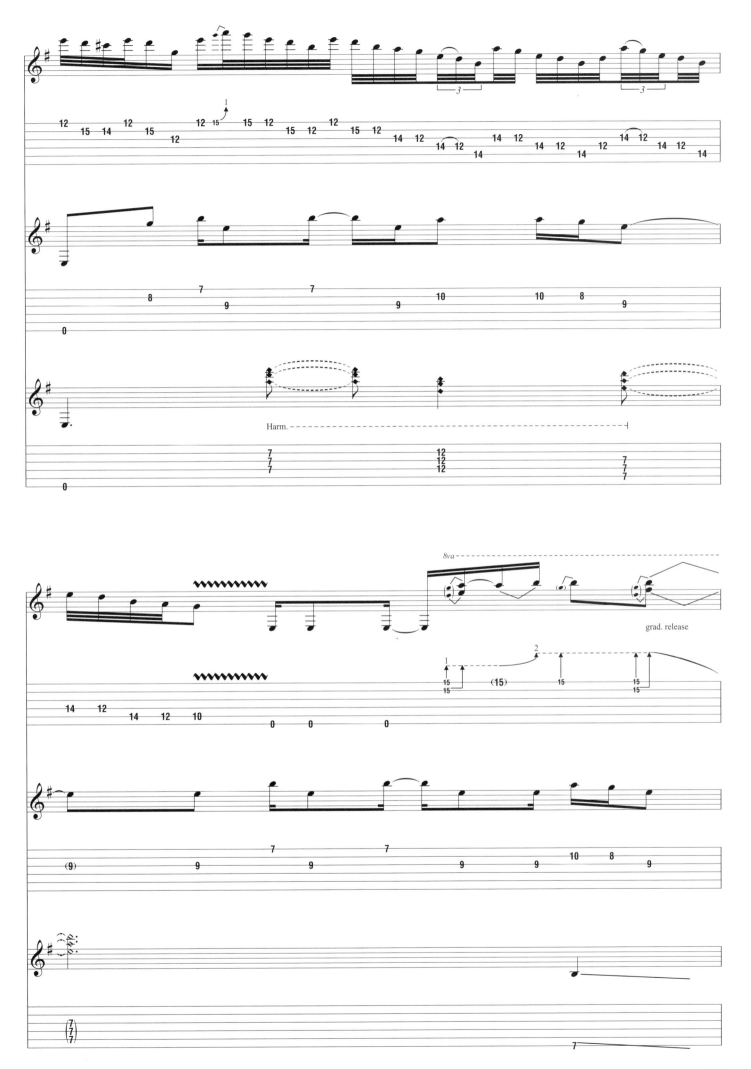

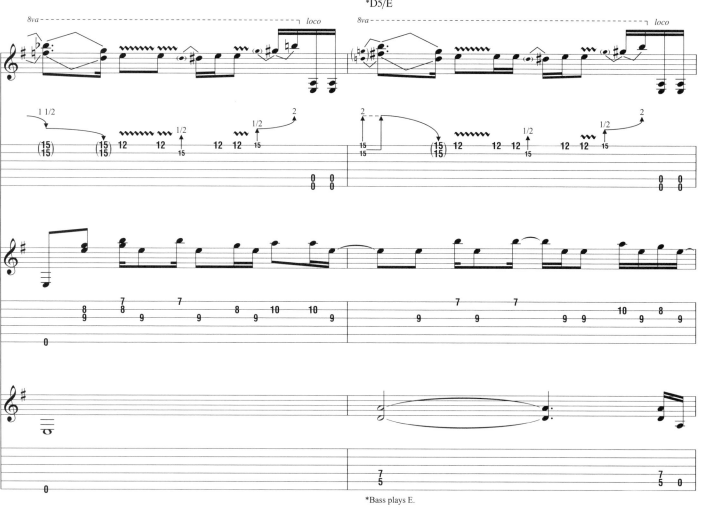

*Bass plays E.

A/E   B5/E   D5/E

*Chord symbol reflects combined harmony.

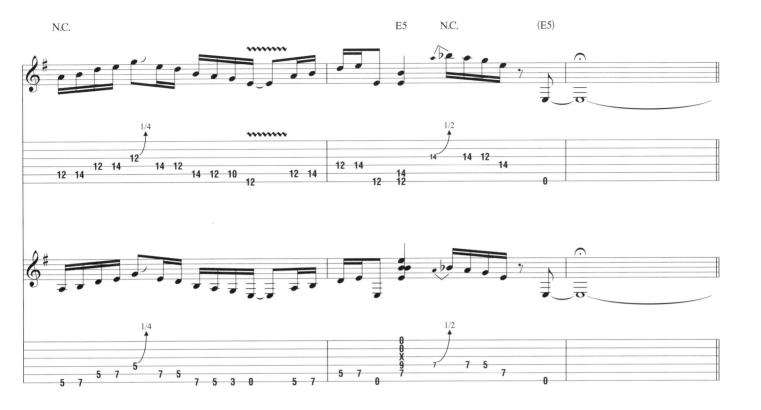

Verse
Free time

N.C.(E5)

3. Oh,   beau-ti-ful,   if you were _ mine, _____   I would write you let-ters ___ and   pour   you sweet wine.

Gtrs. 1, 2 & 3

Gtrs. 1, 2 & 3 tacet
N.C.

Oh, __   beau-ti-ful, ___   why you so __   blue? _   If you can   on-ly   see _____   the   way   I   see you.

from Vance Joy - *Dream Your Life Away*

Riptide

Words and Music by Vance Joy

Intro
Moderately slow ♩ = 97

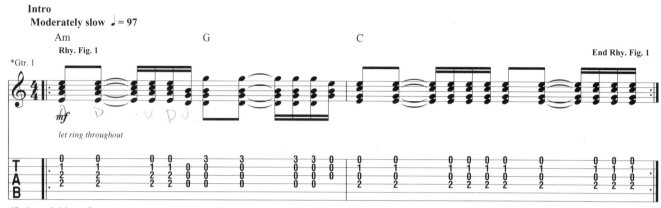

*Baritone ukulele arr. for gtr.
To match recording, tune up 1/2 step.

Verse

Gtr. 1: w/ Rhy. Fig. 1 (4 times)

1. I was scared of den - tists and — the dark. _____   I was scared of pret - ty girls _ and
2. There's this mov - ie that _ I think you'll like. ___   This guy de - cides _ to quit his job _ and

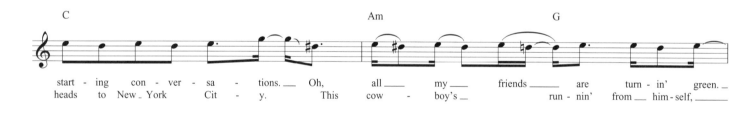

start - ing con - ver - sa - tions. ___ Oh, all ___ my ___ friends _____ are turn - in' green.
heads to New _ York Cit - y. This cow - boy's _ run - nin' from _ him - self,

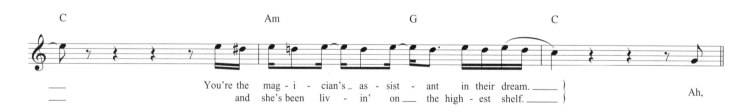

___ You're the mag - i - cian's _ as - sist - ant in their dream. ___
___ and she's been liv - in' on _ the high - est shelf. _____ Ah,

Pre-Chorus

Gtr. 1: w/ Rhy. Fig. 1 (1 1/2 times)

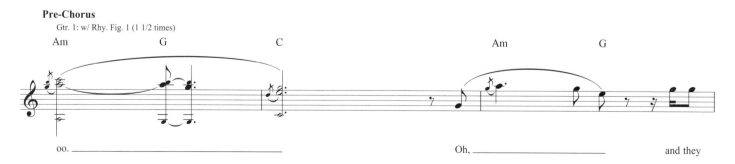

oo. _____   Oh, _____ and they

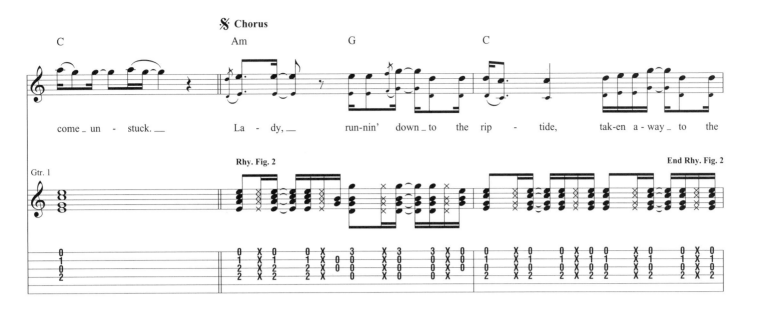

Chorus

come — un - stuck. — La - dy, — run-nin' down — to the rip - tide, tak-en a - way — to the

1st, 2nd & 4th times, Gtr. 1: w/ Rhy. Fig. 2 (3 times)
3rd time, Gtr. 1: w/ Rhy. Fig. 2 (2 1/2 times)

dark side. I wan - na be — your left — hand — man. — I love you when you're sing - ing that

To Coda 2 ⊕   To Coda 1 ⊕

song — and I got a lump — in my throat 'cause you're gon - na sing — the words ——— wrong.

Interlude

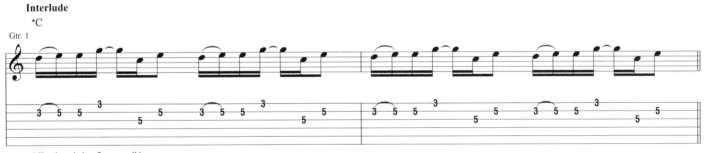

*Chord symbols reflect overall harmony.

Bridge

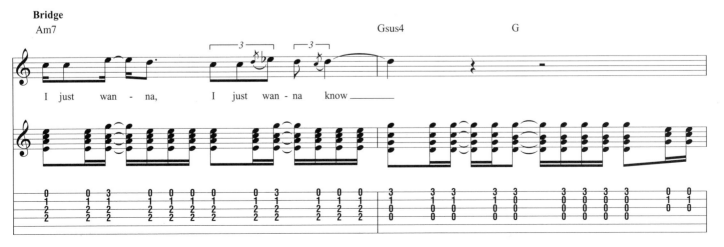

I just wan - na, I just wan - na know ———

63

Chorus

from Ed Sheeran - *X*

Sing

Words and Music by Ed Sheeran and Pharrell Williams

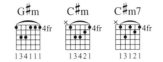

Ig - nor - in' ev - 'ry-bod - y here,___ we ___ wish they would dis - ap-pear ___ so may - be

we could get ___ down, ___ now. _____

End Rhy. Fig. 2

End Rhy. Fig. 2A

End Riff A

69

then, we got noth-in' to say___ and noth-in' to know but some-thin' to drink___ and may-be some-thin' to smoke.

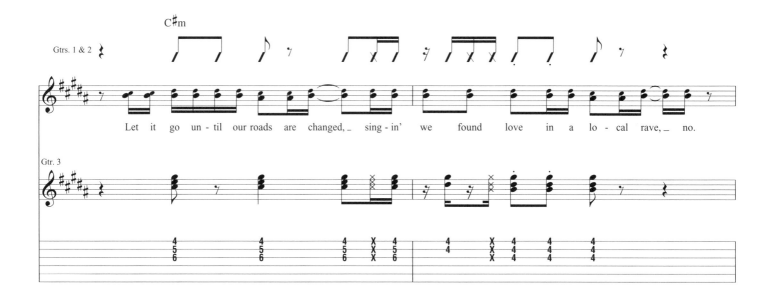

C#m

Gtrs. 1 & 2

Let it go un-til our roads are changed,___ sing-in' we found love in a lo-cal rave,___ no.

Gtr. 3

Gtrs. 1 & 2: w/ Rhy. Fig. 2 (last 2 meas.)
Gtr. 3: w/ Rhy. Fig. 2A (last 2 meas.)

I don't real-ly know what I'm sup-posed to say,___ but I can just fig-ure it out and hope and pray.___ I

Gtrs. 1 & 2: w/ Rhy. Fig. 2
Gtr. 3: w/ Rhy. Fig. 2A

G#m

told her my name.___ I said, "It's nice to meet___ you." Then she hand-ed me a bot-tle of wa-ter with te-qui-la.

I al-read-y know it, she's a keep-er just from this one small act of kind-ness. I'm in

C#m

deep. If an-y-bod-y finds out, I meant___ to drive home but I drank all of it, now. Not

D.S. al Coda

so-ber-ing up, we just sit on the couch.___ One thing___ led to an-oth-er, now she's kiss-in' my mouth. I

Coda

(Can you feel __

Bridge

Gtrs. 1 & 2: w/ Rhy. Fig. 1

G#m

All the guys in here don't e-ven wan-na dance. __

All that I can hear is mu-sic from the back.

__ it?

Can you feel _____ it? __

Can you feel __

C#m7

Rhy. Fig. 4

End Rhy. Fig. 4

Gtrs. 1 & 2

Found you hid-in' here, so won't you take my hand, __ dar-lin', be-fore the beat kicks in a - gain? Can you feel __

__ it?)

Gtr. 7 (acous.)

mf

P.M. throughout

Gtr. 6 (acous.)

mf

P.M. throughout

Gtr. 5 (acous.)

mf

P.M. throughout

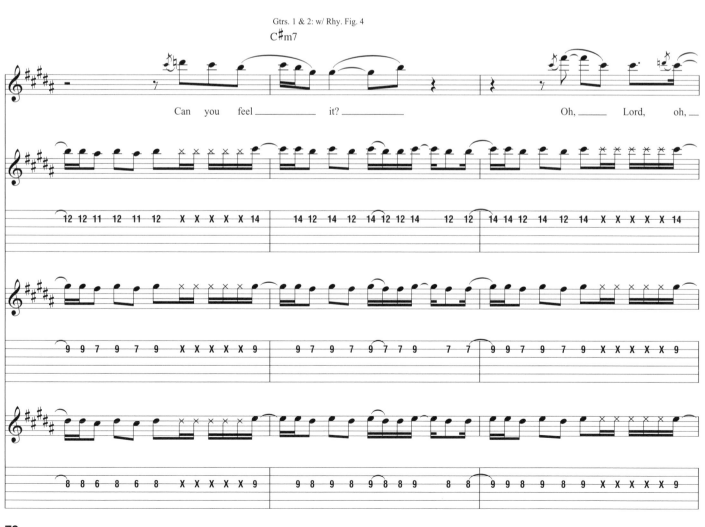

no, ____ whoa, ____ oh, lo, ____ lo.

Sing!

I

Outro-Chorus

Bkgd. Voc.: w/ Voc. Fig. 1 (3 1/2 times)
Gtrs. 1 & 2: w/ Rhy. Fig. 3 (1 3/4 times)
Gtr. 3: w/ Rhy. Fig. 2A (2 times)
Gtr. 4: w/ Riff A (2 times)
Gtrs. 5, 6 & 7 tacet

G#m

Loud - er!

need you, dar - ling, come on set the tone. If you feel you're fall - in', won't you let me know? Ho, ____

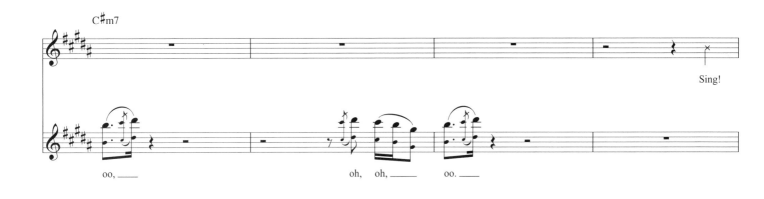

oo, _____   oh,   oh, _____   oo. _____

If   you   love ___ me, come on,   get   in - volved. _   Feel   it   rush - in' through _ you from your

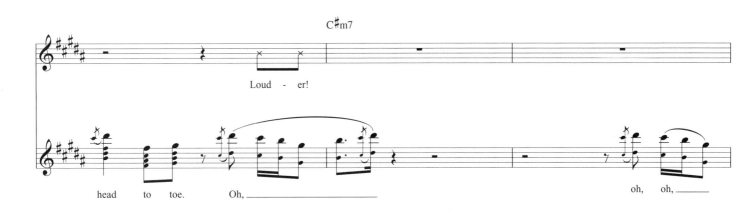

Loud - er!   oh,   oh, _____

head   to   toe.   Oh, _____

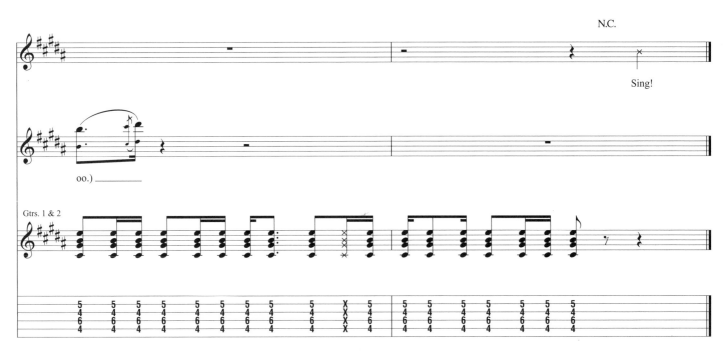

oo.) _____

Gtrs. 1 & 2

from Foo Fighters - *Sonic Highway*

Something from Nothing

Words and Music by Dave Grohl, Taylor Hawkins, Nate Mendel, Chris Shiflett and Georg Ruthenberg

Gtr. 9: Baritone gtr. tuning:
(low to high) A-E-A-D-F♯-B

Intro
Moderately slow ♩ = 92

*Em

Gtr. 1 (clean)

mp
w/ fingers
let ring throughout

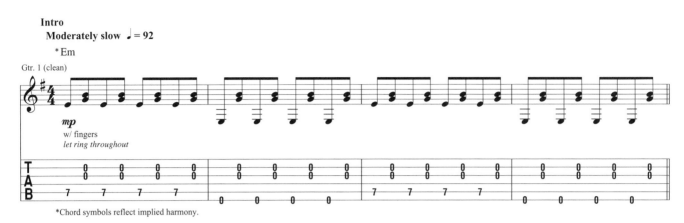

*Chord symbols reflect implied harmony.

Verse

Em   G+/D♯   G/D

1. Give me the flam-ma-ble ___ life. _____   I'm cold as a ___ match _____   read-y to ___ strike. _

Rhy. Fig. 1

C♯m7♭5   Cmaj7   Em   A7sus2

_____   So here   I _____ go. ___

End Rhy. Fig. 1

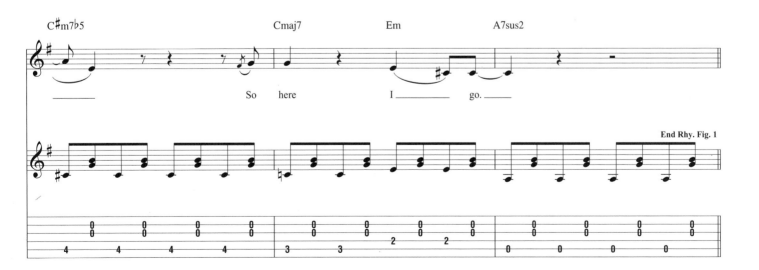

Verse

Gtr. 1: w/ Rhy. Fig. 1

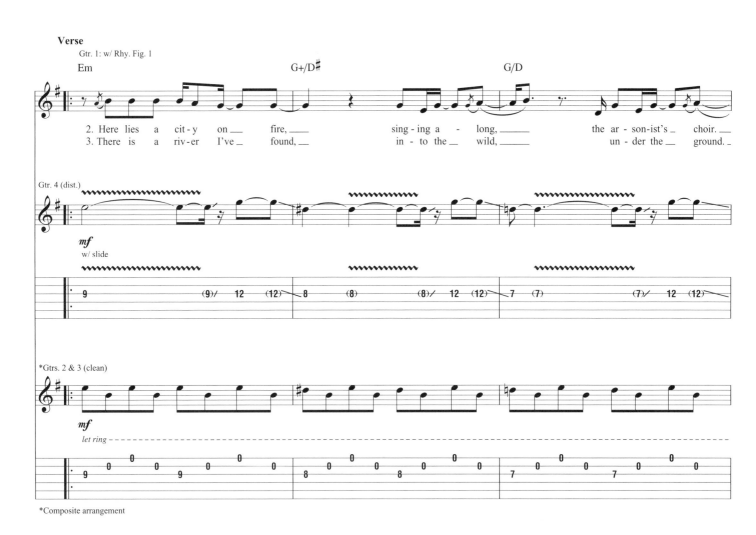

2. Here lies a cit-y on ___ fire, ___ sing-ing a - long, ___ the ar - son-ist's ___ choir. ___
3. There is a riv-er I've ___ found, ___ in - to the ___ wild, ___ un - der the ___ ground. ___

Gtr. 4 (dist.)

mf
w/ slide

Gtrs. 2 & 3 (clean)

mf
let ring - - - - - - - - - - - - -

*Composite arrangement

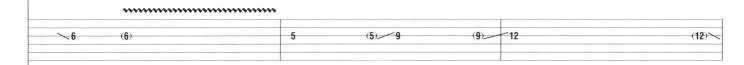

C♯m7♭5   Cmaj7   Em   A7sus2

Now   here   I   go. ___
So   here   I   go. ___

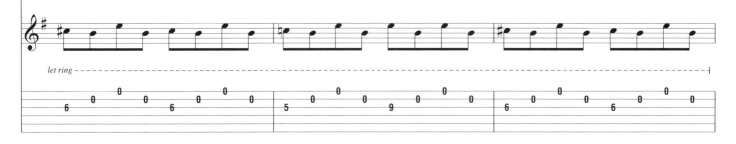

let ring -

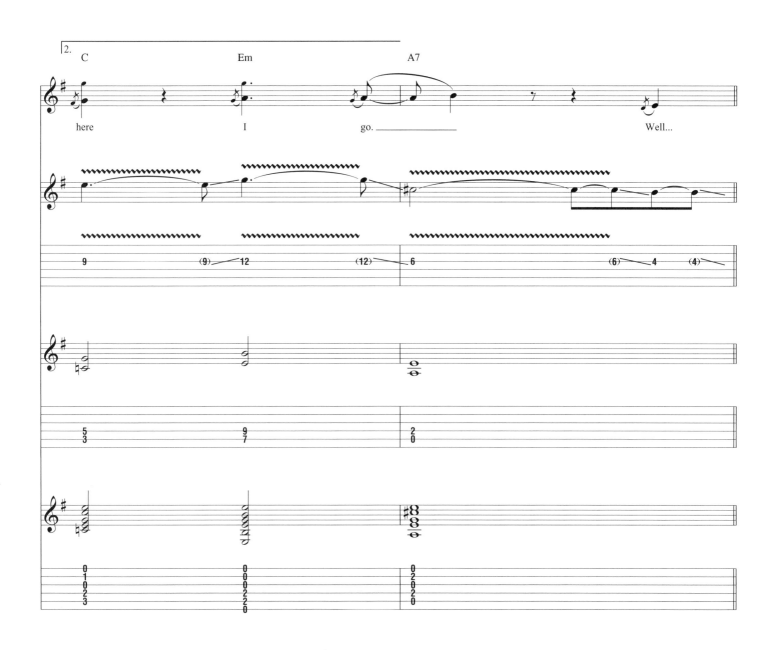

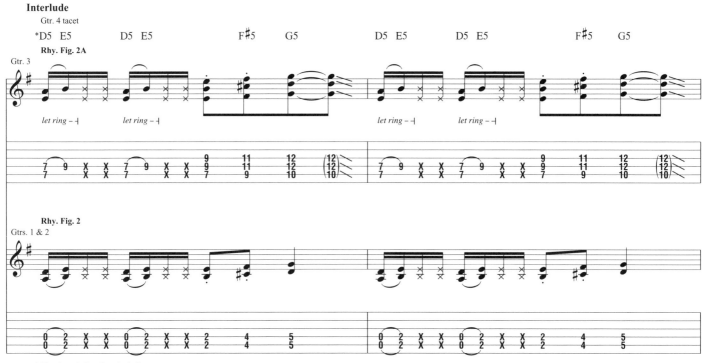

*Chord symbols reflect basic harmony.

Verse

Gtrs. 1 & 2: w/ Rhy. Fig. 2
Gtr. 3: w/ Rhy. Fig. 2A

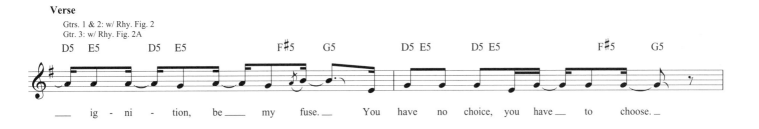

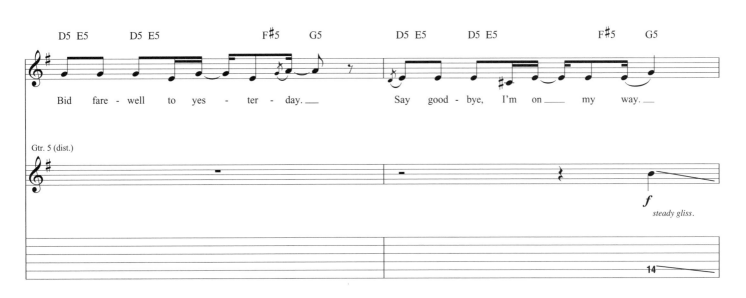

But in ___ the end, ___ we all ___

*Rick Nielsen

Bridge

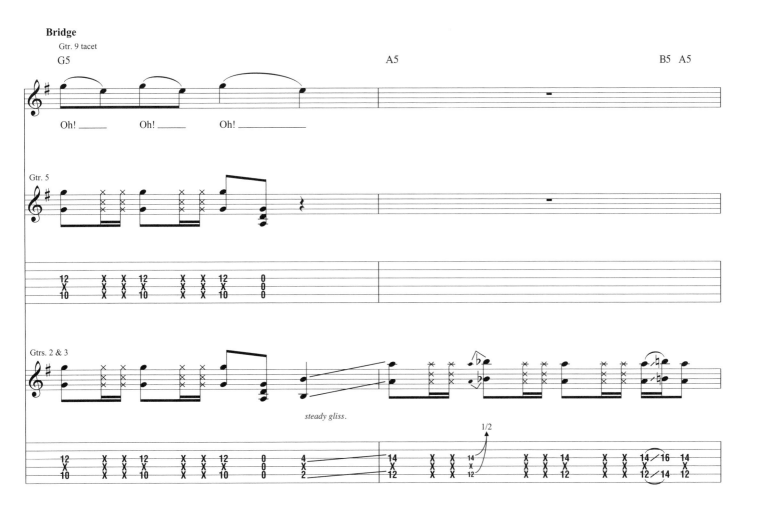

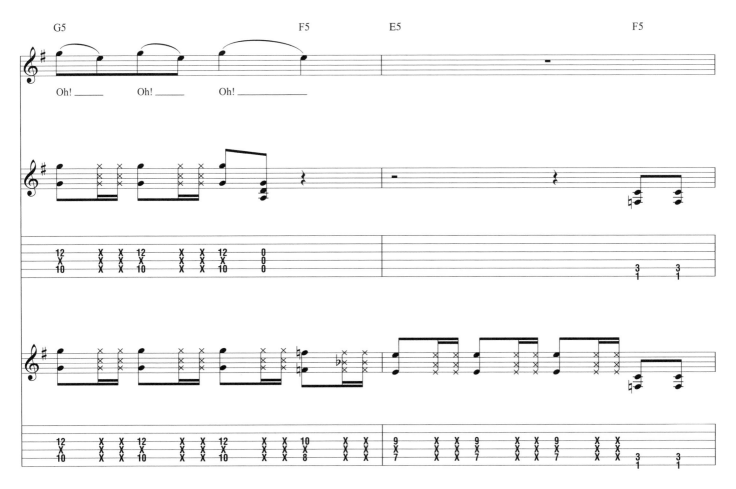

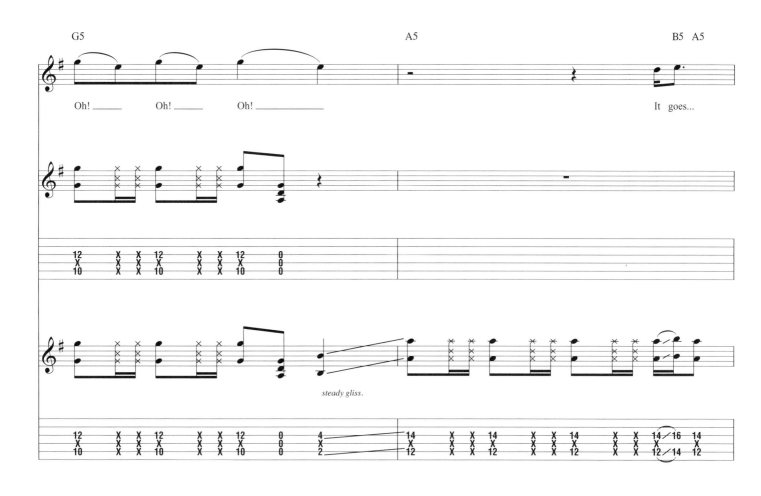

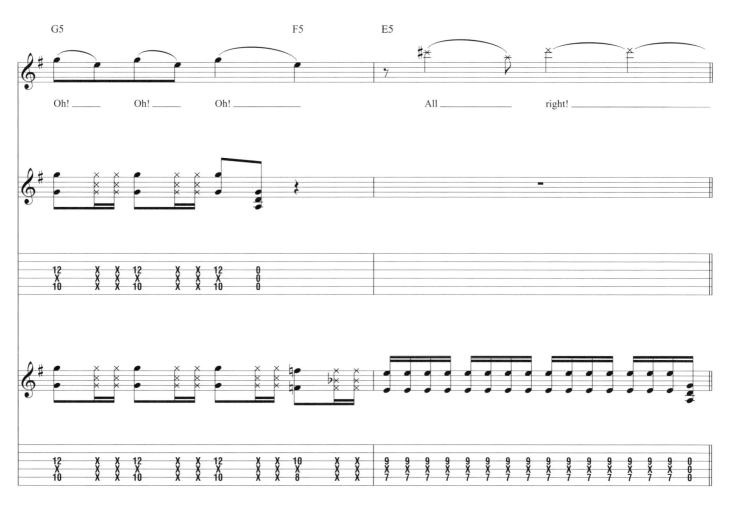

Interlude
Double-time feel

Gtrs. 2 & 5: w/ Rhy. Fig. 2
Gtr. 3: w/ Rhy. Fig. 2A (2 times)

*Microphonic fdbk., not caused by string vibration.

89

Outro-Chorus

Gtr. 3: w/ Rhy. Fig. 4

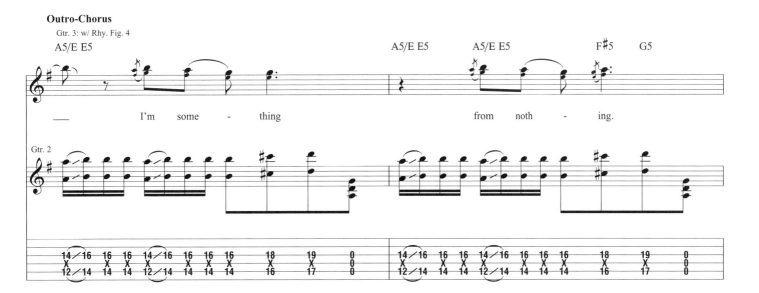

End double-time feel

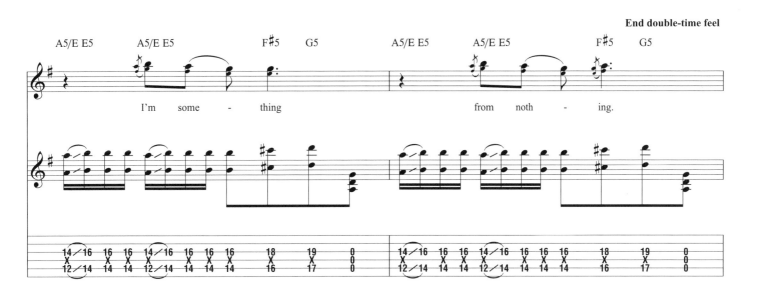

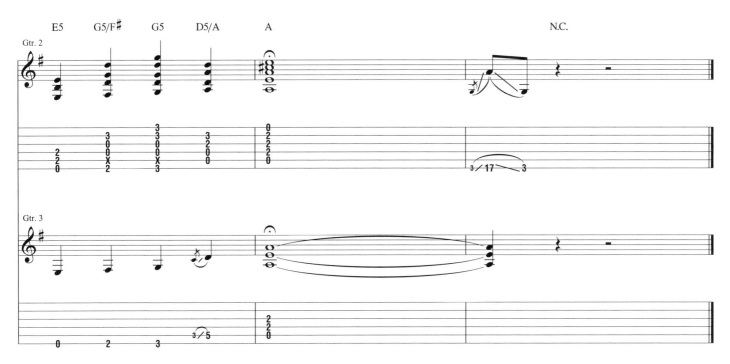

from Milky Chance - *Sadnecessary*

Stolen Dance
Words and Music by Clemens Rehbein

Tune down 1/2 step:
(low to high) E♭-A♭-D♭-G♭-B♭-E♭

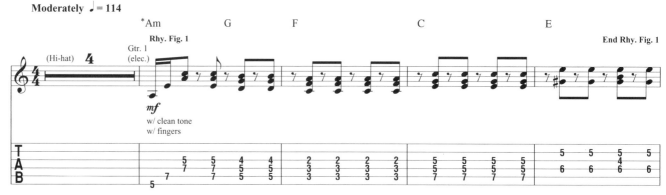

*Chord symbols reflect implied harmony.

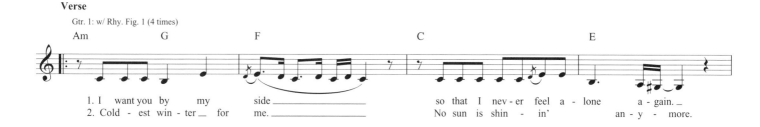

1. I want you by my side ____ so that I nev-er feel a - lone a - gain. ____
2. Cold - est win-ter ____ for me. ____ No sun is shin - in' an - y - more.

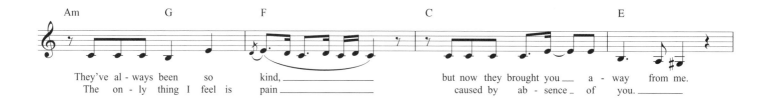

They've al - ways been so kind, ____ but now they brought you ____ a - way from me.
The on - ly thing I feel is pain ____ caused by ab - sence ____ of you. ____

I hope they did - n't get your mind. ____ Your heart is too strong an - y - way.
Sus - pense con - trol - lin' ____ my mind. ____ I can - not find the way out - ta here.

We need to fetch back ____ the time ____ they have sto - len ____ from us.
I want you by my side ____ so that I nev - er feel a - lone a - gain. ____

Gtr. 1

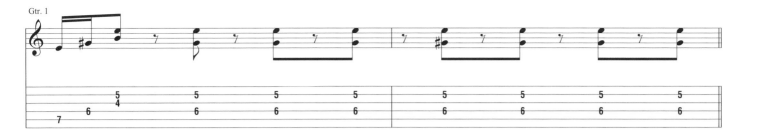

𝄋 **Chorus**

Gtr. 1 tacet

I want you. We can bring it on ___ the floor. I've nev - er

Riff A
Gtr. 3 (elec.)

mf
w/ clean tone & chorus
w/ fingers
let ring throughout

Rhy. Fig. 2
Gtr. 2 (acous.)

mf
w/ fingers

danced ___ like this be - fore. ___ We don't talk a - bout ___ it.

End Riff A

End Rhy. Fig. 2

Gtr. 2: w/ Rhy. Fig. 2 (2 3/4 times)
Gtr. 3: w/ Riff A (2 3/4 times)

Danc - in' on, do the boog - ie all ___ night long. Stoned ___ in par - a - dise, ___

___ should - n't talk a - bout ___ it. I want you. We can bring it on ___ the floor. I've nev - er

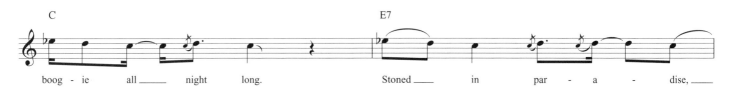

danced ___ like this be - fore. _____ We don't talk a - bout ___ it. Danc - in' on, do the

boog - ie all ___ night long. Stoned ___ in par - a - dise, ___

To Coda ⊕

___ should - n't talk a - bout ___ it, should - n't talk a - bout ___ it. _____

Gtr. 3

Gtr. 2

Interlude

Gtr. 1: w/ Rhy. Fig. 1 (2 times)
Gtrs. 2 & 3 tacet

Am   G   F

Riff B

Gtr. 4 (elec.)

mp

w/ clean tone
P.M. throughout

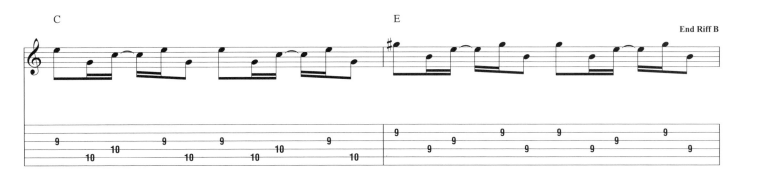

2nd time, D.S. al Coda

Gtr. 4: w/ Riff B

Am   G   F   C   E

Coda

Outro

Gtr. 1: w/ Rhy. Fig. 1
Gtr. 4: w/ Riff B

Am   G   F   C   E

Play 4 times

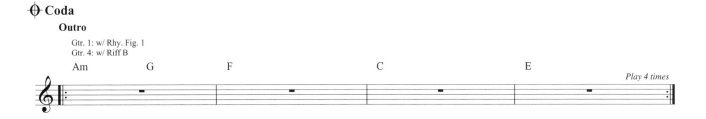

Play 3 times and fade

Am   G   F   C   E

Gtr. 1

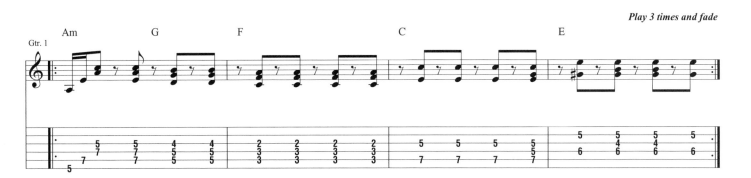

from Colbie Caillat - *Gypsy Heart*

Try

Words and Music by Colbie Caillat, Jason Reeves, Antonio Dixon and Kenneth Edmonds

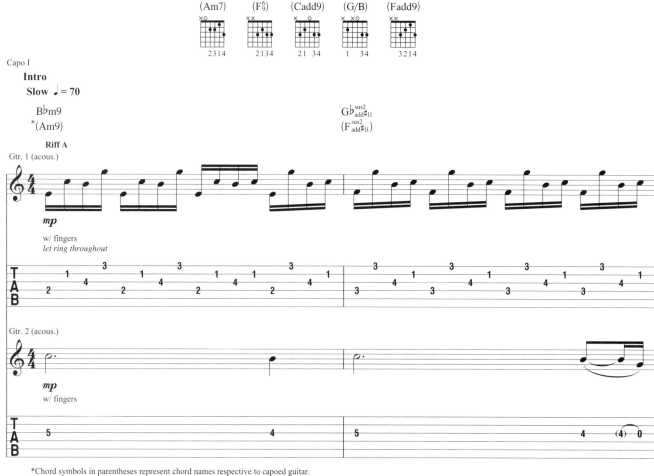

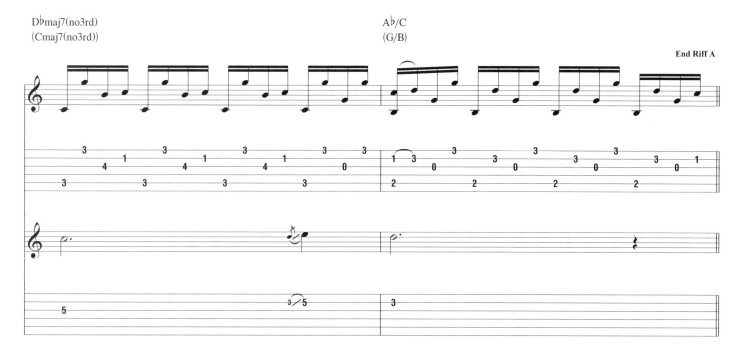

*Chord symbols in parentheses represent chord names respective to capoed guitar.
Symbols above reflect actual sounding chords. Capoed fret is "0" in tab.
Chord symbols reflect implied harmony.

Verse

Gtr. 1: w/ Riff A (2 times)
Gtr. 2 tacet

1. Put your make-up on, get your nails done, curl your hair, run the ex-tra mile, keep it slim so they like you. _

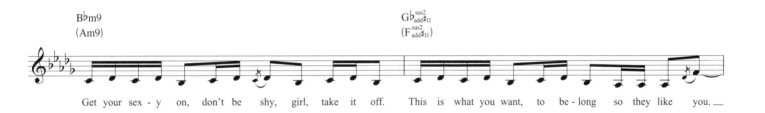

_ So they like you. _

Get your sex-y on, don't be shy, girl, take it off. This is what you want, to be-long so they like you. _

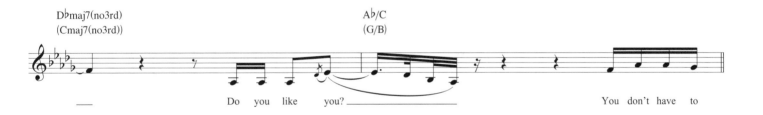

_ Do you like you? _ You don't have to

Pre-Chorus

try so _ hard. You don't have to give it all a-way. _ You just have to

*See top of first page of song for chord diagrams pertaining to rhythm slashes.

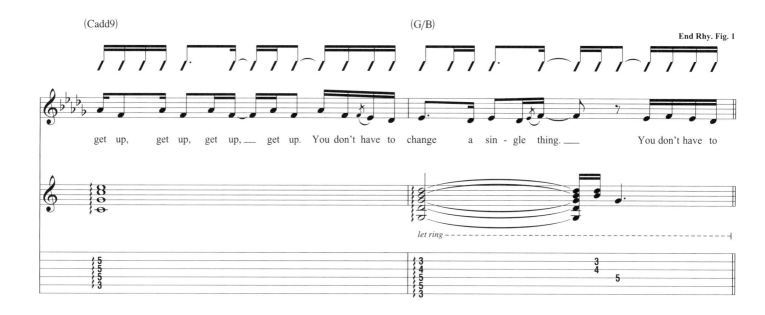

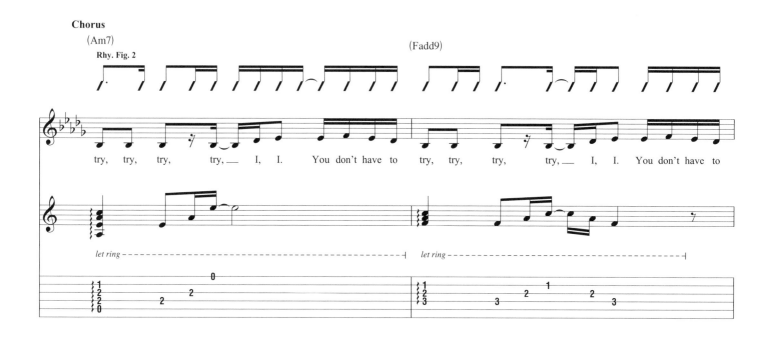

Chorus

D♭add9
(Cadd9)

A♭/C
(G/B)

get up, get up, get up,___ get up. You don't have to change a sin-gle thing.___ You don't have to

Chorus

B♭m7
(Am7)

G♭add9
(Fadd9)

try, try, try, try,___ I, I. You don't have to try, try, try, try,___ I, I. You don't have to

*Gtrs. 1 & 2

*Composite arrangement

D♭add9
(Cadd9)

A♭/C
(G/B)

try, try, try, try,___ I, I. You don't have to try. No, you don't have to

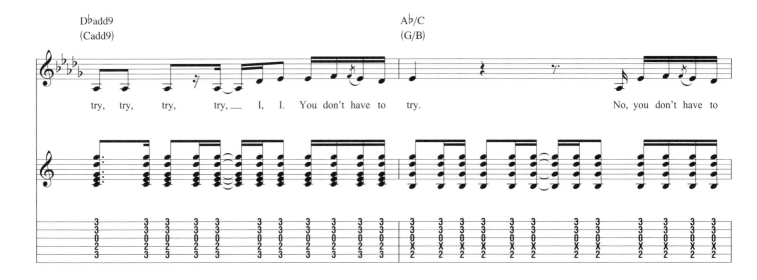

Gtrs. 1 & 2: w/ Rhy. Fig. 2

B♭m7
(Am7)

G♭add9
(Fadd9)

try, try, try, try,___ I, I. You don't have to try, try, try, try,___ I, I. You don't have to

D♭add9
(Cadd9)

A♭/C
(G/B)

try, try, try, try,___ I, I. You don't have to try. You _____ don't have to

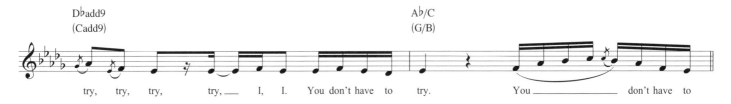

Interlude

Gtr. 1: w/ Riff A

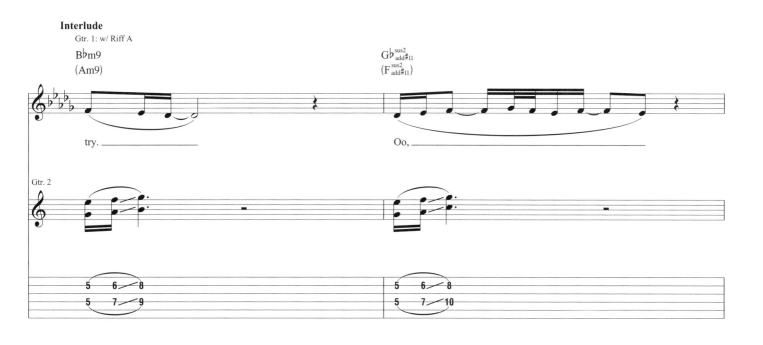

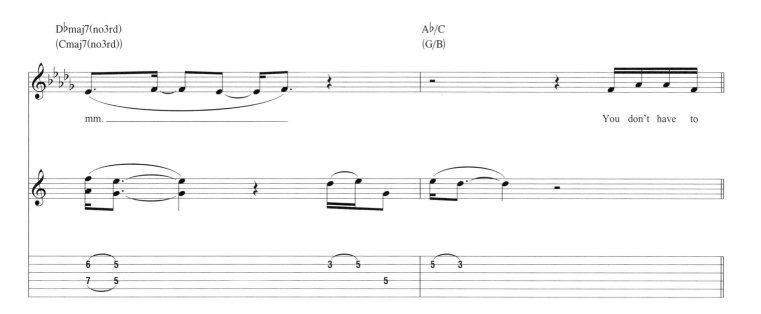

Pre-Chorus

*Composite arrangement

from Slash - *World on Fire*

World on Fire

Words and Music by Saul Hudson and Myles Kennedy

Tune down 1/2 step:
(low to high) Eb-Ab-Db-Gb-Bb-Eb

Intro

Very fast ♩ = 175

*A7

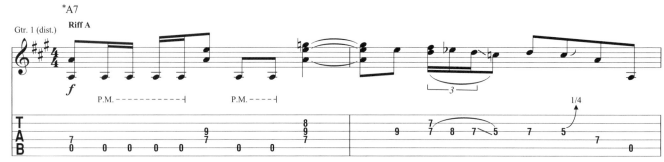

*Chord symbols reflect implied harmony.

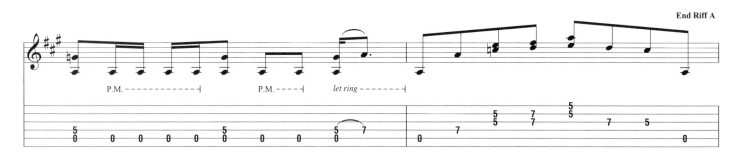

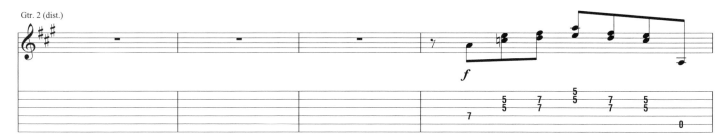

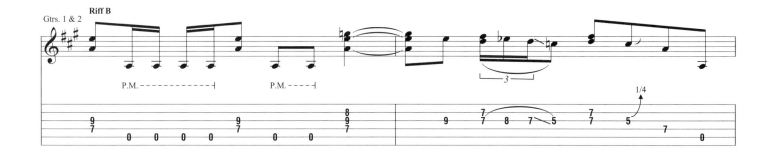

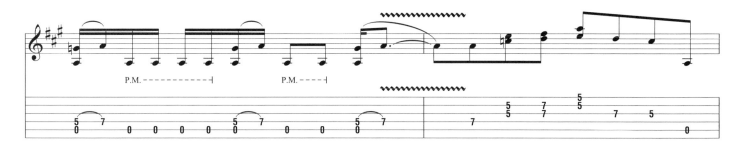

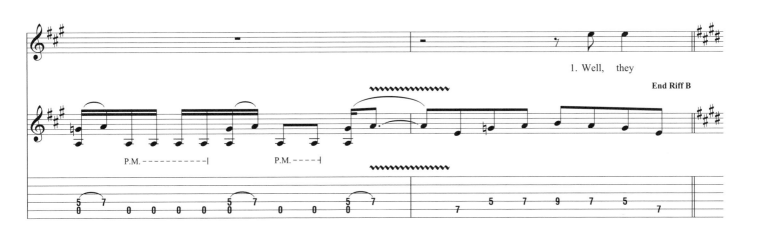

1. Well, they

End Riff B

Verse

E7

say that we ___ are trag - ic and they say ___ we're born to lose. ___ You're the mis -
like a new re - li - gion, speak in tongues, ___ come see the light. ___ Do not trip ___

Riff C

End Riff C

Gtrs. 1 & 2: w/ Riff C (3 times)

- fit, I'm the sin - ner. You're the heath - en, I'm the fool. ___ But to - day ___
___ on in - hi - bi - tions that will on - ly waste ___ my time. ___ Let me tempt ___

___ you'll be the mas - ter or the slave, ___ it's up to you. ___ Oh, my beau -
___ you with ___ the ev - ils of the flesh ___ and so much more. ___ Like a Bab -

- ti - ful ___ dis - as - ter, take me an - y way you choose. ___
- y - lon re - deem - er, like a push - er, like a whore. ___

Pre-Chorus

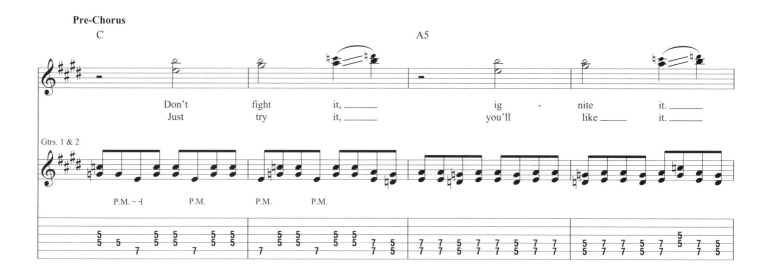

Don't   fight   it, _____   ig -   nite   it. _____
Just   try   it, _____   you'll   like _____ it. _____

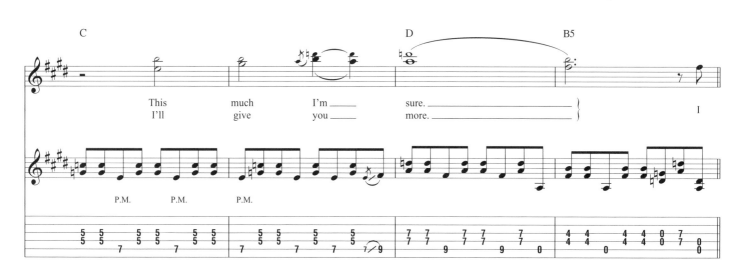

This   much   I'm _____ sure. _____   I
I'll   give   you _____ more. _____

𝄋 Chorus

think   it's   time   to   set   this   world   on   fire. _____   I
                                (This   world   on   fire. _____

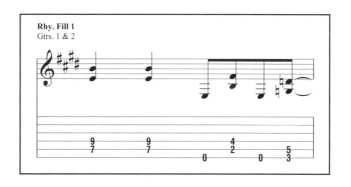

think it's time to push it to ___ the edge. ___   To ___ the edge. ___

3rd time, Gtrs. 1 & 2: w/ Rhy. Fill 2

1., 2. Burn it to the ground ___ and trip the wire. ___
3. I'm so fuck-ing bored ___ so trip the wire. ___
Just trip the wire.) ___   It may nev-

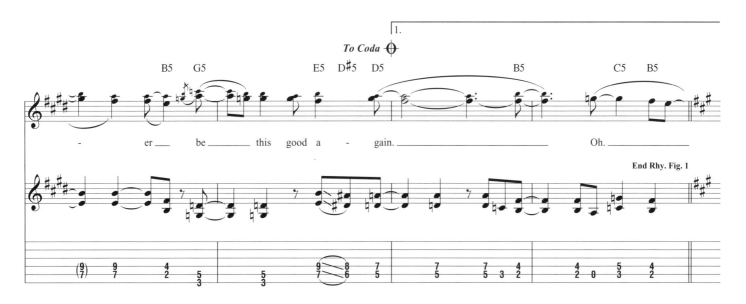

To Coda ⊕

-er ___ be ___ this good a - gain. ___ Oh. ___

End Rhy. Fig. 1

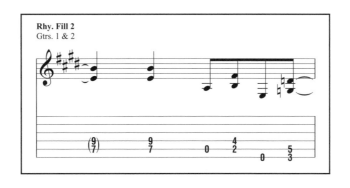

Rhy. Fill 2
Gtrs. 1 & 2

Interlude

Gtrs. 1 & 2: w/ Riff B

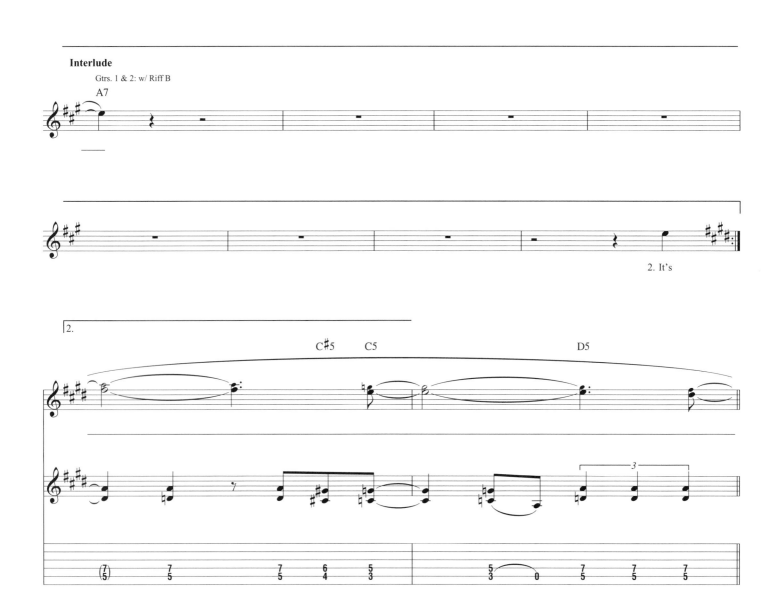

2. It's

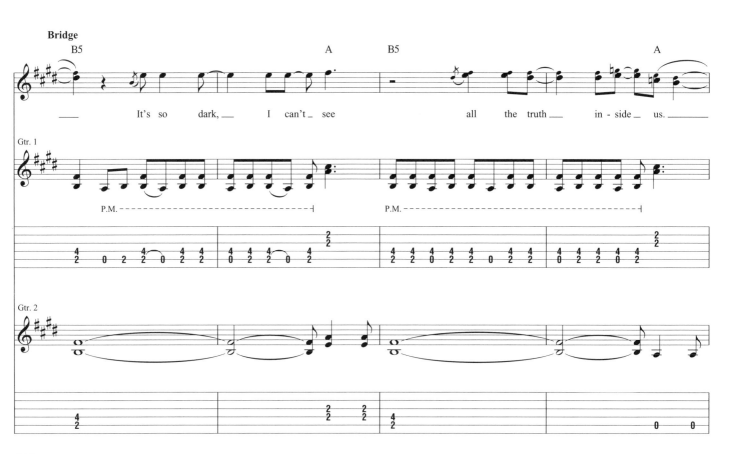

It's so dark, __ I can't __ see all the truth __ in - side __ us. __

All I want is to feel some - thing that's real before the end.

Guitar Solo

Gtrs. 1 & 2: w/ Rhy. Fig. 1

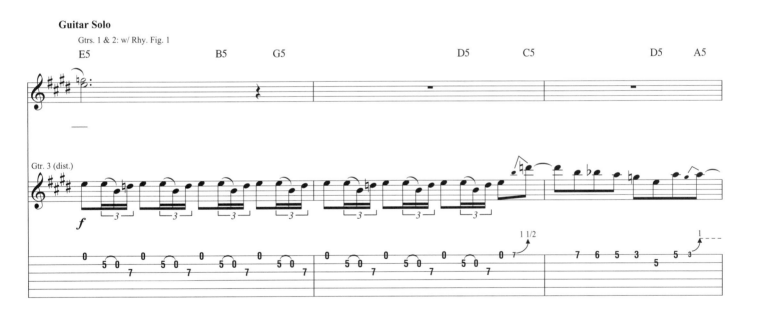

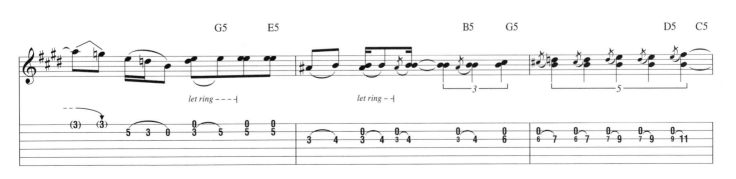

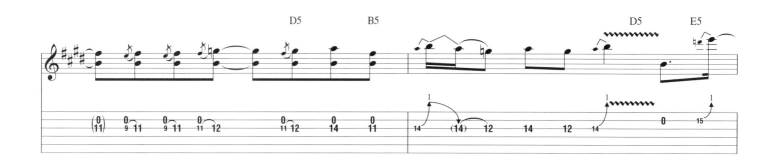

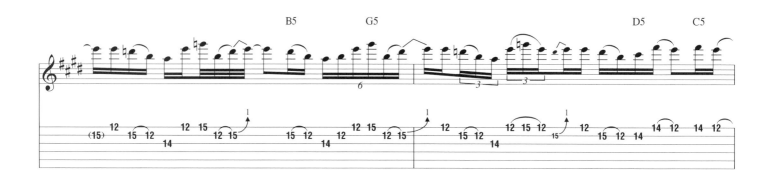

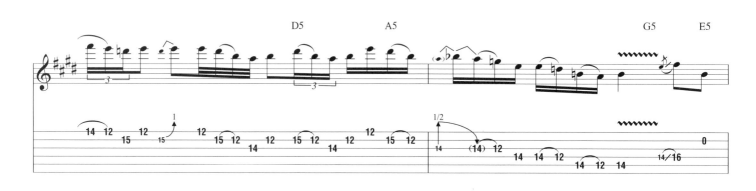

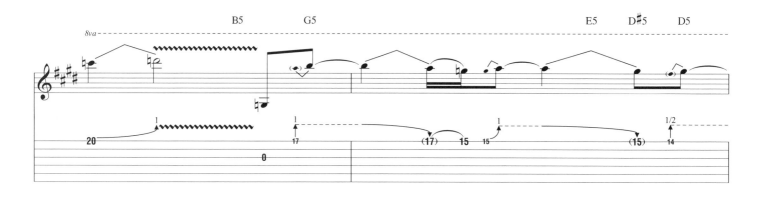

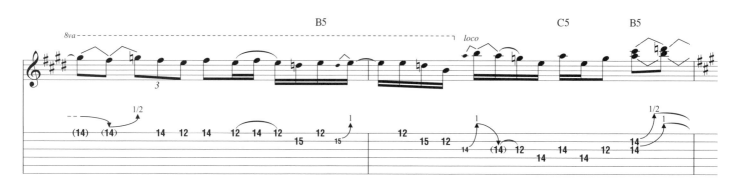

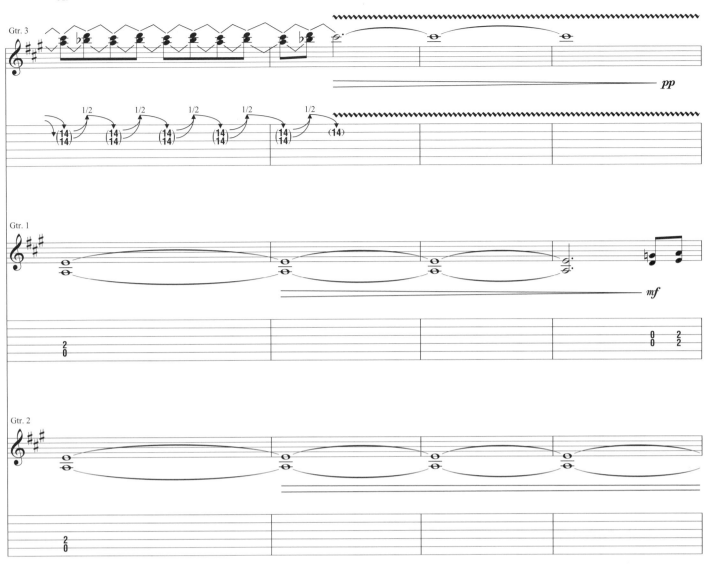

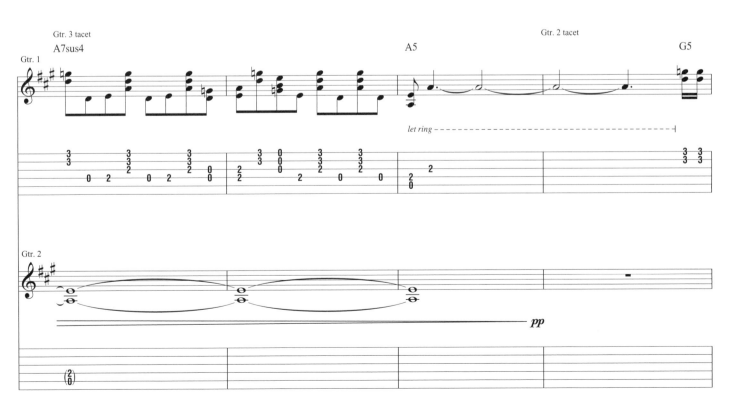

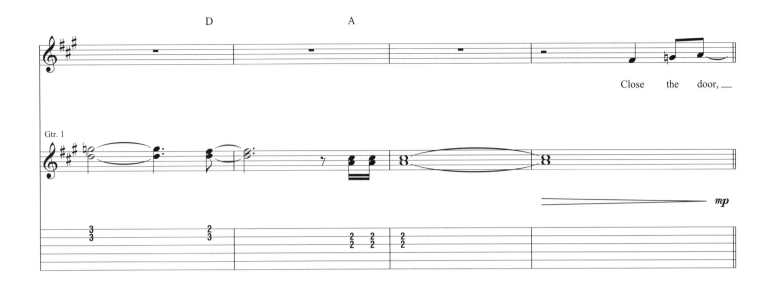

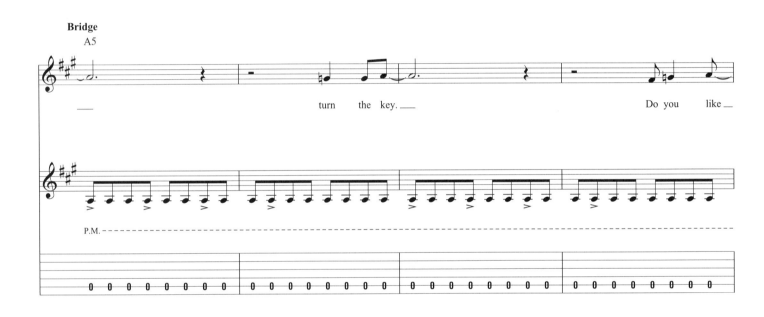

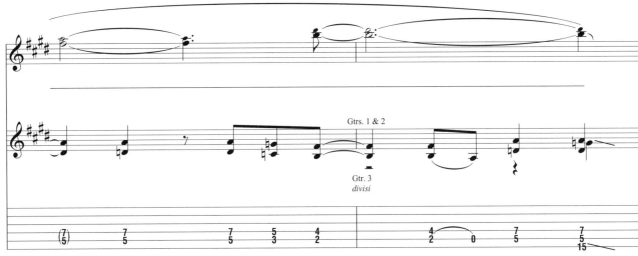

Outro-Guitar Solo

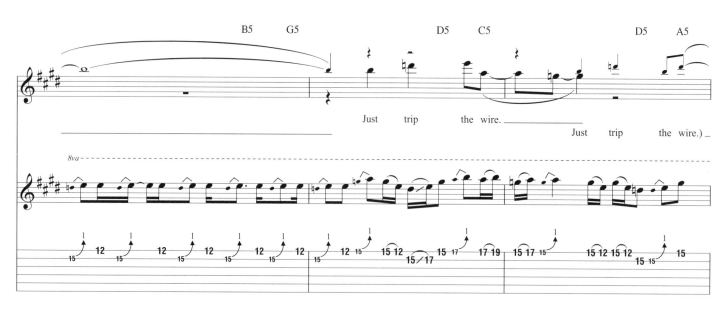

It may nev - er be ___ this good a - gain. ___

GUITAR NOTATION LEGEND

Guitar music can be notated three different ways: on a *musical staff*, in *tablature*, and in *rhythm slashes*.

RHYTHM SLASHES are written above the staff. Strum chords in the rhythm indicated. Use the chord diagrams found at the top of the first page of the transcription for the appropriate chord voicings. Round noteheads indicate single notes.

THE MUSICAL STAFF shows pitches and rhythms and is divided by bar lines into measures. Pitches are named after the first seven letters of the alphabet.

TABLATURE graphically represents the guitar fingerboard. Each horizontal line represents a string, and each number represents a fret.

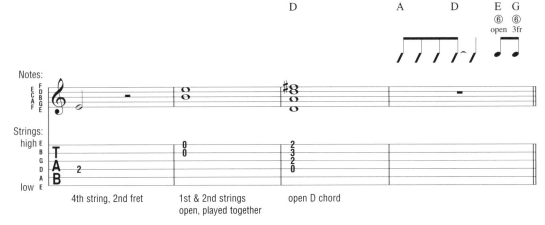

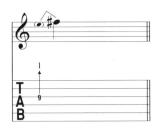

4th string, 2nd fret   1st & 2nd strings open, played together   open D chord

Definitions for Special Guitar Notation

HALF-STEP BEND: Strike the note and bend up 1/2 step.

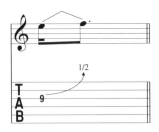

WHOLE-STEP BEND: Strike the note and bend up one step.

GRACE NOTE BEND: Strike the note and immediately bend up as indicated.

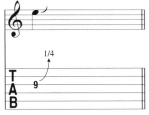

SLIGHT (MICROTONE) BEND: Strike the note and bend up 1/4 step.

BEND AND RELEASE: Strike the note and bend up as indicated, then release back to the original note. Only the first note is struck.

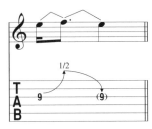

PRE-BEND: Bend the note as indicated, then strike it.

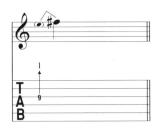

PRE-BEND AND RELEASE: Bend the note as indicated. Strike it and release the bend back to the original note.

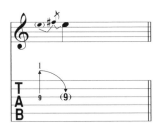

UNISON BEND: Strike the two notes simultaneously and bend the lower note up to the pitch of the higher.

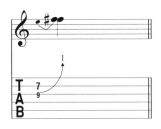

VIBRATO: The string is vibrated by rapidly bending and releasing the note with the fretting hand.

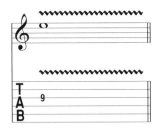

WIDE VIBRATO: The pitch is varied to a greater degree by vibrating with the fretting hand.

HAMMER-ON: Strike the first (lower) note with one finger, then sound the higher note (on the same string) with another finger by fretting it without picking.

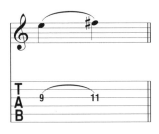

PULL-OFF: Place both fingers on the notes to be sounded. Strike the first note and without picking, pull the finger off to sound the second (lower) note.

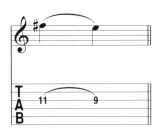

LEGATO SLIDE: Strike the first note and then slide the same fret-hand finger up or down to the second note. The second note is not struck.

SHIFT SLIDE: Same as legato slide, except the second note is struck.

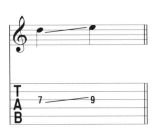

TRILL: Very rapidly alternate between the notes indicated by continuously hammering on and pulling off.

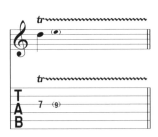

TAPPING: Hammer ("tap") the fret indicated with the pick-hand index or middle finger and pull off to the note fretted by the fret hand.

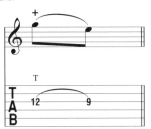

NATURAL HARMONIC: Strike the note while the fret-hand lightly touches the string directly over the fret indicated.

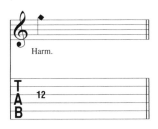

Harm.

PINCH HARMONIC: The note is fretted normally and a harmonic is produced by adding the edge of the thumb or the tip of the index finger of the pick hand to the normal pick attack.

P.H.

HARP HARMONIC: The note is fretted normally and a harmonic is produced by gently resting the pick hand's index finger directly above the indicated fret (in parentheses) while the pick hand's thumb or pick assists by plucking the appropriate string.

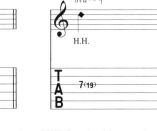

H.H.

PICK SCRAPE: The edge of the pick is rubbed down (or up) the string, producing a scratchy sound.

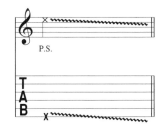

P.S.

MUFFLED STRINGS: A percussive sound is produced by laying the fret hand across the string(s) without depressing, and striking them with the pick hand.

PALM MUTING: The note is partially muted by the pick hand lightly touching the string(s) just before the bridge.

P.M. - - - - - - - - - - - -

RAKE: Drag the pick across the strings indicated with a single motion.

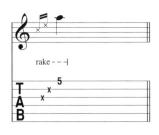

rake - - ┤

TREMOLO PICKING: The note is picked as rapidly and continuously as possible.

ARPEGGIATE: Play the notes of the chord indicated by quickly rolling them from bottom to top.

VIBRATO BAR DIVE AND RETURN: The pitch of the note or chord is dropped a specified number of steps (in rhythm), then returned to the original pitch.

w/ bar

VIBRATO BAR SCOOP: Depress the bar just before striking the note, then quickly release the bar.

w/ bar - - - - - - - - - ┤

VIBRATO BAR DIP: Strike the note and then immediately drop a specified number of steps, then release back to the original pitch.

w/ bar - - - - - - - - - - ┤

Additional Musical Definitions

(accent)	• Accentuate note (play it louder).	

(accent)	• Accentuate note with great intensity.	

(staccato)	• Play the note short.	

■   • Downstroke

V   • Upstroke

D.S. al Coda   • Go back to the sign (𝄋), then play until the measure marked "***To Coda***," then skip to the section labelled "**Coda**."

D.C. al Fine   • Go back to the beginning of the song and play until the measure marked "***Fine***" (end).

Rhy. Fig.   • Label used to recall a recurring accompaniment pattern (usually chordal).

Riff   • Label used to recall composed, melodic lines (usually single notes) which recur.

Fill   • Label used to identify a brief melodic figure which is to be inserted into the arrangement.

Rhy. Fill   • A chordal version of a Fill.

tacet   • Instrument is silent (drops out).

• Repeat measures between signs.

• When a repeated section has different endings, play the first ending only the first time and the second ending only the second time.

NOTE: Tablature numbers in parentheses mean:
    1. The note is being sustained over a system (note in standard notation is tied), or
    2. The note is sustained, but a new articulation (such as a hammer-on, pull-off, slide or vibrato) begins, or
    3. The note is a barely audible "ghost" note (note in standard notation is also in parentheses).

RECORDED VERSIONS®

The Best Note-For-Note Transcriptions Available